BRETT SHUNKWILER

YOUR
FINANCIAL
PATHWAY
FOR
RETIREMENT

The Road to Getting
and Staying Retired

All rights reserved. No part of this publication may be reproduced, distributed or transmitted in any form or by any means, including photocopying, recording, or other electronic or mechanical methods, without the prior written permission of the publisher, except in the case of brief quotations embodied in critical reviews and certain other noncommercial uses permitted by copyright law. For permission requests, contact the publisher.

Phone: 402.466.3919
Fax: 402.464.0648
Email: info@shunkwilerfinancial.com

Visit the author online:www.shunkwilerfinancial.com

Your Financial Pathway for Retirement—Brett Shunkwiler, 1st ed.

ISBN 9798667116097

Representative of and securities and investment advisory services offered through Brokers International Financial Services, LLC. Member SIPC. Brokers International Financial Services, LLC and Shunkwiler Financial are not affiliated companies.

We are an independent financial services firm helping individuals create retirement strategies using a variety of investment and insurance products to custom suit their needs and objectives. Investing involves risk, including the potential loss of principal. No investment strategy can guarantee a profit or protect against loss in periods of declining values. None of the information contained in this book shall constitute an offer to sell or solicit any offer to buy a security or any insurance product.

Any references to protection of benefits or steady and reliable income streams refer only to fixed insurance products. They do not refer, in any way, to securities or investment advisory products. Annuity guarantees are backed by the financial strength and claims-paying ability of the issuing insurance company. Annuities are insurance products that may be subject to fees, surrender charges and holding periods which vary by product and insurance company. Annuities are not FDIC insured.

Not associated with or endorsed by the Social Security Administration or any other government agency.

Shunkwiler Financial does not offer legal or tax advice. Please consult the appropriate professional regarding your individual circumstance.

TABLE OF CONTENTS

Chapter One - Retirement, Finally; Now What Do I Do? 1

Chapter Two - The Retirement Transition: When Every Day Is Saturday 7

Chapter Three - Income Planning: The Foundation Of Retirement Planning 13

Chapter Four - Investment Planning: Know Your Limits In Retirement 33

Chapter Five - Tax Planning: How Much Will Be Yours To Keep? 49

Chapter Six - Health Care Planning: Getting Older Can Be Expensive 69

Chapter Seven - Legacy Planning: Leaving A Part Of You That Lives On 81

Chapter Eight - Pick Your Guide On The Pathway For Retirement 91

About The Author 97

Acknowledgments 99

CHAPTER ONE

Retirement, Finally; Now What Do I Do?

*T**he finish line is finally in sight. All those years spent running in the rat race—a.k.a., the grind of the everyday working world—are nearly over. Hard as it once seemed to imagine, I'm finally getting ready to retire.*

It's a great feeling, no doubt about it. I've spent more than forty years working long and hard, all the while planning for and looking ahead to this time that once seemed like a distant dream. Yet, now this dream is about to become a reality, I can't seem to shake a strange, new-found feeling of . . . What? Apprehension? Uncertainty? Fear of the unknown?

I guess what I'm really asking is, "What do I do now?"

Welcome to the world of retirement. My name is Brett Shunkwiler, and I'm a registered investment advisor representative and retirement planner based in Lincoln, Nebraska. Through this book, I hope to help guide you into a new world, in an experience that has the potential to be one of the most exciting journeys of your life. Yet, this occasion is one some people approach with the kind of trepidation expressed at the opening of the chapter.

My team at Shunkwiler Financial hears these sentiments daily from first-time visitors who come to see us. We talk every day with people who have spent thirty, thirty-five, forty, or more years in the workforce and now either look forward to a day when they no longer have to work or have already moved into retirement.

Most of these good folks have done an excellent job of saving for their retirement futures. Many will come into our office for a first meeting with a variety of different accounts. In addition to their checking and savings accounts, coupled with a CD or two, they are likely to have a 401(k) or 403(b), and possibly one or more individual retirement accounts (IRA). They may have assorted stocks, bonds, and mutual funds in a brokerage account. Some may have an annuity contract or two, and maybe one or more life insurance policies. At times, these various accounts start to resemble a toolbox, the place where a lot of useful "stuff" is stored and often forgotten. Over time, it's easy to lose track of what you have or don't have there.

I applaud and appreciate these people for their foresight and wisdom. They've had their eye on the prize that is their retirement.

And yet, some of these same people often have little understanding about how to turn these assets and savings into income—real cash—in retirement. This is where my team enters the picture.

We're happy to find most of our first-time visitors have done well in saving for their future. But we ask tough but essential questions:

- Do you know with 100 percent certainty that you have enough assets to produce a sustainable and increasing stream of income that will maintain your current standard of living throughout your lifetime?
- Which of your many accounts do you plan on pulling from first when you need income in retirement, and why?
- Have you thought about your Social Security and when to begin taking it as part of an integrated plan that includes all of your other financial assets?
- Have you thought about the taxability of your current accounts and if it might be a good idea to convert some of your tax-deferred accounts into tax-free accounts?
- Have you considered how to deal with the rising health care costs that inevitably come along as we grow older? Do you have a plan to deal with the potentially significant expenses associated with long-term care? Do you know there are other ways to help assist with long-term care expenses other than spending hundreds of

dollars a month on a traditional long-term care policy? Would you like to know about the other options available to help offset those costs?

It's at this point that we often get more blank stares than answers. You can almost sense their wheels beginning to turn as our visitors consider these pivotal issues.

Then there are the inevitable questions people ask of us.

"Have I really saved enough for retirement, a period that might last twenty, twenty-five, thirty, or more years? Can I really afford to retire in a year, two years, three? Will I have to take a part-time job in retirement to make ends meet? Worse yet, will I have to work longer than I want to? Will I have enough to leave something for my surviving spouse and other loved ones?"

And then, the biggest question of all: "Will my retirement assets last as long as I do with inflation figured in?"

THE LIFELONG EMPHASIS ON ACCUMULATION

Please don't misunderstand me here. I don't mean to be critical in suggesting that many of us don't have all the information we need as we prepare to enter or already are in retirement—a world different from anything we knew in the daily workforce.

It's not hard to explain why this happens.

So much of the financial services industry, especially as presented in TV ads and promotional material, is built around the sale of investment products. Not that this doesn't make financial sense. Let's be real: If one doesn't amass retirement assets and savings during the "accumulation phase" of our lives, there is no financial income in the "distribution phase" that comes with retirement. The failure to accumulate during our workplace years can create a world of hurt—one none of us want to experience when it comes time to turn our assets into income/cash.

At the same time, though, some of the people we meet—those who did exactly what the financial services industry urged them to do by investing in themselves and their futures during their working years—have done little planning for generating income in the years when they no longer receive a regular paycheck. They've assembled a toolbox of retirement assets, but don't necessarily know how these different financial tools must work together to complete the project—that is, building a full-fledged, long-lasting retirement income plan.

Some people don't fully realize, for example, how much income they will have or need in retirement. They are confused about taking Social Security benefits, especially when it comes to the most advantageous time to start taking those benefits. They may have little knowledge of what to do with their 401(k) or 403(b) retirement plans that have been administered by their employers over the years, but which they will have the responsibility to control. They are not completely sure how an annuity produces income, or exactly what kind of benefits a life insurance policy could provide them or a surviving spouse or other family members.

And like many Americans of all ages, they may not fully realize the potential effect of taxes on their future income. Moreover, they might not realize how taxes will be different in retirement than they were in the working years.

UNDERSTANDING THE DISTRIBUTION PHASE OF LIFE

I started this book with the opinion that many people who've done a good job in the accumulation phase of their lives—the times when we provide for growing families while saving what we can when we can for a time in the future—get far too little advice when it comes to income planning in the distribution part of life, the years when we should be enjoying retirement.

That's why in the upcoming chapters we hope to provide some insight on the full spectrum of retirement planning.

We'll talk about income planning and filling the "income gap"—the difference between regular living expenses and regular fixed income—by turning retirement assets into retirement income that has the potential to last throughout one's life.

We'll also examine ways to provide 1) asset growth coupled with 2) protection against loss of value due to market volatility and 3) tax-efficient income in retirement. Those are all important considerations when planning in the years just before and during retirement.

We'll also look at tax strategies designed to help keep more money in your pocket as opposed to Uncle Sam's. Then we'll address health care planning, including alternatives for long-term care coverage. And finally, we'll look at legacy and estate planning, the necessary process of providing for surviving loved ones.

We also will discuss "volatility control," an issue of concern for many people during the 2020 coronavirus panic that saw the stock market plummet from bull market record highs in February to bear market lows just five weeks later. We'll talk about the importance of developing an income plan that includes reliable, sustainable streams of income that are not tied to the rise and fall of the market.

These elements are the core of Shunkwiler Financial's Pathway for Retirement™ process. Over the course of this book, we will demonstrate how each piece is essential to our retirement planning approach. Working cohesively, these components can provide a more defined picture of what we can expect in our well-deserved years away from the daily grind of the workforce—the time when we finally become our own employer in retirement.

5 COMPONENTS OF THE SHUNKWILER FINANCIAL PATHWAY FOR RETIREMENT™

1) Income planning
2) Investment planning
3) Tax planning
4) Health care planning
5) Legacy planning

LET'S TALK PROCESS, NOT PRODUCTS

You should know in advance that this will not be a book for hot stock tips or recommendations on the best investment tools—a.k.a., "retirement investing."

Accumulating retirement assets is important, no doubt. But equally important is having a long-range income plan that allows you to know your financial future isn't dependent on the market growing at a 20 percent rate each year. Developing such a plan involves a process as much as it does the financial products that are part of that process.

This book will map out what I believe to be the essential concepts in "retirement planning," something different and much more complex than "retirement investing."

CHAPTER TWO

The Retirement Transition: When Every Day Is Saturday

I tend to think of our retirement years as having three distinct phases. Let's call them the go-go, slow-go, and no-go phases.

The "go-go" phase of retirement can be, and should be, one of the most exciting periods of our lives.

The first ten or so years of retirement can be a wonderful transition period from the stress, politics, and grind of the everyday working world into a new time when every day is like a Saturday. These are the years when you can still be on the run, though now at a pace of your choosing.

Most people during this time—and here's hoping you are among them—still have relatively good health and can do the things they've put off doing for years. They no longer have to wait for weekends and vacations to engage in leisure, recreational, and volunteer activities. They now have the opportunity to travel or spend more time with friends and family. They can take on new interests and projects, or just have the time to enjoy the simple pleasures of life—walking the dog, taking a nap, reading a book—at any time and place of their choosing.

And yes, there can still be a place for compensated employment. The big difference in retirement, however, is that the goal now is to continue working, preferably on a part-time or consulting basis, only because you want to and not because you have to.

There will come a time later in retirement when health issues are likely to make us tap the brakes to decelerate into the "slow-go" years. These typically come ten to twenty years into retirement, when we no longer move as fast or care to travel as much as we did in the first decade of retirement.

Eventually, time takes an even greater toll on our bodies and we enter the "no-go" phase. These are the years we stay at home more, when instead of visiting loved ones we encourage them to visit us. Yet, even in these advanced stages of life, the goal remains the same as in the go-go years. That is, to have income that enables us to live the lifestyle we choose, not one imposed on us.

CAN I AFFORD TO HAVE OPTIONS?

Our financial health also will be a factor in how we approach the three phases of retirement. We want to be able to afford to have options, a goal of any long-term retirement plan.

We want to know, for instance, that we have the financial ability to retire at a time of our choosing should the stress and strain of a job leave us looking longingly at the exit every day, counting the minutes until 5 p.m. We want to know we can afford to take an occasional cruise or be a snowbird in Arizona or Florida during our harsh Nebraska winters. We want to know we can afford to travel for the graduations or weddings of grandkids, or just to see old friends in faraway places. We want to know, should serious health issues necessitate nursing care, we won't be a burden to our loved ones.

No doubt, there are many aspects of retirement we look forward to with great anticipation. But there are other aspects of the working world we are going to miss upon leaving it.

We may miss the company of co-workers who have become close friends. We may miss the familiarity of a regular schedule. We may miss the challenge that comes with doing a job the way we know it must be done.

Above all else, we are going to miss that regular paycheck.

One of the most common things we hear from people preparing for or in the first years of retirement is the fear of the unknown. Much of that concern involves the ability to maintain a consistent, dependable income upon which they can live the retirement lifestyle of their dreams.

"We've never had to worry much about paying our bills; we've typically earned more than we spend," first-time visitors often tell us. "But we worry that this might change once we no longer get a regular paycheck."

It's a valid concern, but one that can be addressed with the development of a sustainable income plan that tells us precisely where our new "retirement paycheck" will come from.

We know, for instance, that there will be reliable income from Social Security, the government pension fund/safety net we've been paying into ever since we first learned that something called FICA was taking withholding payments from our first paycheck. We'll talk about Social Security options in more detail in the next chapter.

Some fortunate people—primarily public service employees like the many clients we see from the University of Nebraska-Lincoln or the State of Nebraska—might also have pension income. (Congratulations if you will receive this benefit, something that is a disappearing species in the private sector.) Some people may also have rental income, dividend income, inheritance income, and, yes, possible part-time employment income in retirement.

This is what people commonly call their "fixed income." It's a principal component on the credit side of the income vs. expense equation that is part of any income plan for both working and retired families alike. To make this equation balance, a family must also have a decent estimation of their regular expenses.

We will talk in more detail about income planning in the next chapter.

But let's first talk about something you must consider in any discussion of the transition from your working years to retirement. That is, how much income will you want or need in retirement?

DON'T CHEAT YOURSELF

We often hear visitors say, usually during a preliminary discussion of income vs. expenses in retirement, that they are not especially concerned about having less income after they stop receiving a regular paycheck.

"We'll be all right," they might say, "because we plan to live on less in retirement."

Really? Is that the way it works?

Let's look at this idea a bit more closely.

We talked earlier in this chapter about how every day in retirement can feel like a Saturday (or whatever day of the week was yours to control). That's a nice thought, but let's also consider this:

Back when you were working Monday through Friday, on what day of the week were you inclined to spend the most money?

The answer for many people is Saturday (or whatever day of the week was your day off). Most of us likely spent more money on days when recreation, family activities, dining out, or weekend excursions commanded our attention. "I live for the weekend" is more than the title of a song by Triumph.[1]

Now let's ask another question. Now that retirement is either approaching or is finally here, now that you have 365 Saturdays each year, do you really expect to spend less money than you did in your working years? Put another way: Did you really spend thirty-five, forty, or more years on the job so you would have a reduced standard of living in retirement?

I don't think you really want that. This is why one goal we have at our financial firm is to help people develop a retirement plan that enables them to enjoy the same standard of living—or maybe even a little higher—especially in the "go-go" years of retirement when we are generally in better physical shape to enjoy this new phase of life.

---

[1] Yeah, I know; Triumph isn't on my playlist, either. I had to Google them. They were a Canadian hard-rock band of the late 'seventies and 'eighties. And now you know.

You've spent your life working hard for this time. You deserve a chance to reward yourself. Go ahead, live a little.

The challenge in retirement planning is to develop lifelong streams of income that, with adjustments for inflation, can supplement our fixed income (Social Security, etc.) and allow us to maintain the lifestyles we desire in retirement.

For most readers of this book, this means using some of the assets from the retirement nest egg you spent a lifetime building. Most people have saved and planned for retirement and now look for ways to employ their retirement assets in an efficient manner that helps those assets last as long as they live. Many also hope to be able to leave whatever is left of those assets in the most tax-efficient way possible for their loved ones or whomever they choose.

To accomplish these goals requires a plan; it won't happen by chance. We'll spend the upcoming chapter talking about the kind of income planning that can help retirees reach the retirement goals they've set for themselves.

CHAPTER THREE

Income Planning: The Foundation of Retirement Planning

L et's cut right to the million-dollar question on the mind of many people we encounter on a first-time visit to our office.

"What we really need to know is, will I be able to retire now, or relatively soon, and do I have enough money to last as long as I do while keeping the same standard of living, or maybe even improving it with inflation figured in?"

Well, let's start crunching some numbers and see.

WHAT'S YOUR NUMBER?

It would be easier, of course, if there were a Magic Number, a total amount of retirement savings that could guarantee the lifestyle of our dreams. Sorry, but that figure just doesn't exist, despite suggestions you might see in any number of retirement advice forums.

The $1 million figure is frequently tossed around as a target goal for retirement savings. It's a nice round number, easy to understand, but it doesn't guarantee anything other than the thrill of calling oneself a millionaire.

Kudos if you can do that, but the fact remains that one simply can't rely on any single magic number to assure a steady flow of income in retirement. We know of clients who retired with considerably less than $1 million and made their retirement savings last as long or longer than some millionaires who burned through their assets like a Midwest prairie fire.

Two real-life stories help illustrate this "tale of two cities."

Doc and Donna Martin (fictional names for real people) were Omaha physicians in their mid-forties who enjoyed a relatively high income and an equally upscale lifestyle. When we first visited, they had a combined income of around $400,000 annually, but their living expenses ate up most of that. They had revolving credit card debt of around $100,000 a year, yet they were good savers who had amassed about $800,000 in retirement assets.

They thought they were at, or close to, somebody's idea of a magic number, so Donna's first question dealt with whether the two of them might be able to afford an early retirement in about eight years.

After spending some time looking at their lifestyle expenses and examining what they might expect in retirement income, I looked her straight in the eye and gave her news she didn't want to hear.

"More than likely, no, you won't be able to retire as soon as you would like," I told her. "You're spending nearly $400,000 a year. You've saved $800,000, and maybe that number can double in eight years to $1.6 million. But even then, given your current rate of spending and the fact that you won't be eligible for Social Security at your retirement goal of age fifty-five or earlier, you might well run out of money in roughly four to five years of retirement."

Mrs. Martin was shocked. She and her husband had gotten used to spending whatever they wanted whenever they wanted because they had an income that kept pace with their lifestyle. They hadn't, however, taken a close look at life after their regular paychecks stopped arriving. It was a wake-up call she hadn't expected, but that's the hard reality faced by people whose desire for a high standard of living exceeds what they can reasonably expect to receive in retirement income.

Now consider the case of Don and Shirley Jones, fictional names for a real couple from Lincoln.

Don and Shirley were retired and living on a combined income of around $35,000 a year—most of it from Social Security. They retired with around $300,000 in retirement assets. Between the two of them, they worked four part-time jobs, positions they held because they wanted to stay active, not because they needed the extra income.

At the end of each month, Don and Shirley told us they actually were able to put away a little something extra to continue building their retirement nest egg, all while living a lifestyle that gave them the freedom and comfort they wanted.

These two stories are two extreme ends of the retirement income spectrum. But they serve to illustrate the point that a retirement income goal should not be based on some Magic Number, but rather on a detailed look at what you expect to spend and what you expect to receive in income in the years when regular paychecks end.

Please understand something here. Numbers do matter, and we look at a lot of them in drawing up a retirement income plan. The first numbers we consider will determine whether there are reliable income streams in place to support your chosen retirement lifestyle and whether they will last for a lifetime, even with adjustments for inflation. Then we focus on the "fun" numbers that can help you realize experiences that will leave a lasting impression on you and your loved ones. Will you be able to afford that dream trip to Italy? Will you be able to take the grandkids to Disney World? Will you be able to pass along a legacy gift of assets to heirs?

As noted at the beginning of this chapter, some number-crunching is required to determine whether your retirement income can help ensure the kind of life experiences you want to have. Among the numbers that matter most in retirement income planning:

1) What kind of lifestyle expenses, both fixed and discretionary, do you anticipate having in retirement?
2) What level of "fixed income" do you expect from Social Security, a pension, rental property, dividends, or other regular, sustainable income?
3) What kind of supplemental income will you need to fill any gap between those two figures? Beyond that, can you count on taking that income from retirement assets that will last as long or longer than you do?

INCOME PLANNING: IT'S MORE THAN YOUR HOUSEHOLD BUDGET

The key to answering any of the above questions involves income planning, the first critical leg of our Pathway for Retirement™ plan. Income planning is the first step in closing the difference between where you are today and where you hope to be tomorrow. It's where we begin the journey on the road to retirement, or even further into retirement.

The bottom line of any income plan is to see if your retirement assets can create what once was known as "mailbox income," the kind that arrives like clockwork each month (such as Social Security or a pension payment).

In retirement, we need this consistent income flow—just as we did in our working years when it arrived via a regular paycheck—to meet not just our everyday expenses but also the frills we hope to enjoy once we have the time to enjoy them. Admittedly, there likely will be some less-pleasant expenses in our later years. Medical costs and long-term care come most immediately to mind, as might the need to replace a car, a roof, or any other big-ticket expense that comes along in life. A comprehensive retirement income plan must also build in a buffer for both expected and unexpected expenses.

This planning process also deals with choosing how and when to take income from the retirement nest egg we spent years building. What are the most advantageous accounts—based on taxes, market performance, and interest rates—to pull from first? When do we take income from our 401(k), IRA, stocks, bonds, or mutual funds? Is there a plan in place that allows our assets to keep pace with (or stay ahead of) inflation?

Addressing the above questions begins with an estimate of what you expect to have flowing in and what you think will be gushing out, starting with your first years in retirement.

True income planning is much more than budgeting, however. Household budgets deal with bill-to-bill, month-to-month. Retirement income planning, on the other hand, takes a big-picture look over a period of twenty or more years. It establishes a plan by which we know how we will replace the income that disappears when the regular paycheck does. It tells us what amounts of fixed income will be available, and how and when to take additional income from other sources when necessary.

But to fully view that big picture, we must first briefly spend some time weeding through the details of routine budgeting, something that has to be done in order to make intelligent decisions about our income needs.

The first thing to estimate is regular monthly expenses. Begin with recurring items, such as insurance payments for health care and property, all utility bills, a mortgage payment (if any), food and clothing, prescription drug costs, etc. Also include estimates for entertainment, leisure, and travel expenses. (As noted in the previous chapter, plan to have some fun; you've earned it.) You also need to account for what you might be paying annually in taxes, an inevitable expense.

Next, estimate regular monthly income derived from Social Security, a pension (if available), any recurring annuity payments, rental income, and dividends. Factor in employment income if you choose to continue work full time or part-time.

Don't be surprised if expenses exceed income at this stage of the planning process.

This difference is called "the income gap," and filling it is a critical step in the income planning process. This final step involves making the most efficient use of the retirement nest egg you have assembled over a lifetime of hard work. It involves taking income from assets in a tax-efficient and timely manner. It also involves maximizing potential sources of income.

Let's also note that developing a retirement income plan isn't a one-time, one visit thing. Frequent reviews of the plan become necessary as conditions change, especially when new expenses enter the picture.

Some client reviews may indicate a need to cut expenses or create more income. But we also know of reviews in which clients are surprised to learn they are living beneath a lifestyle they can afford. They didn't realize they could be doing more of the fun things they enjoy and are pleasantly surprised when we tell them they can "live" a bit more, take additional trips, use more of the money they have to experience as much of life as they can.

And don't overlook the organizational benefit that can result from this planning.

In putting together a comprehensive income plan, you are gathering up and putting together all the pieces of your financial life, including some elements you may not have paid attention to for years. This assembly process alone can be informative for both an individual and a couple. We visit with many couples in which one spouse handles the household budget while the other keeps track of all investments. One partner sometimes doesn't fully understand what the other is doing, and that can create a special problem, should one spouse pass unexpectedly or become incapacitated. Consider this income-planning project as a way to get both partners involved in a process that can bring their joint financial picture into focus.

A LITTLE DITTY ABOUT JACK AND DIANE

The idea of taking a comprehensive look, possibly for the first time, at our retirement "big picture" can seem daunting to some.

It doesn't have to be.

To be sure, most people who visit our office for the first time arrive with concerns that they haven't saved enough for retirement. Yet after we put together all the widely scattered pieces of their financial lives and describe the retirement income these different assets can generate, many leave with the realization that they are better off than they imagined. Some are pleasantly stunned to learn the retirement date they thought might be a long way down the road is actually right in front of them, available at a time of their choosing.

Those are the good days when we can share this information with an anxious person or couple.

Let's illustrate this discussion with a little ditty about Jack and Diane—with thanks to John Mellencamp for giving fictitious names to some very real clients from America's heartland.

Jack was a postal worker when we first met him. He was worried that he would be delivering mail in Nebraska's torrid summers and icy winters for years longer than he wanted. His body was feeling the effects of years on mail routes; his aching knees cried out for orthopedic surgery. He desperately wanted to retire but was guessing he would have to work two to three more years before doing so.

His wife, Diane, who had not attended our financial seminar that prompted Jack to visit our office, thought her husband was worrying needlessly. "I don't think we need to be here," she said at the start of our first meeting. "I think this is a waste of our time, but Jack wanted me to be here."

As the meeting progressed and we started talking about many of the issues discussed earlier in this chapter, particularly about what specific income the couple might expect from their various investments, you could almost see a light bulb switch on over Diane's head. We were discussing things with which she was familiar, but that she had not completely worked through.

"No one has ever really discussed turning assets into income with me," she said at one point.

Her own advisor, she noted, routinely briefed her on the yearly performance of her IRA investments and sometimes discussed possible adjustments to her portfolio. Yet Diane and her financial professional never had a conversation about how those investments might fit into the couple's retirement income "big picture," which included planning for income, as well as dealing with inflation, health-care expenses and possible long-term nursing care. She began to ask more questions about the five components of our Pathway for Retirement™ plan and quickly realized that she and her advisor had only talked about one, investment planning.

By the end of that first meeting, Diane's outlook had taken a 180-degree turn. When it came time for a second meeting at our office, she brought her own investment statements along with a ton of good questions.

Long story short, at the end of our third meeting, Diane gave me a gigantic hug that I'll never forget. "I've got my husband back," she said. Jack, it seems, was a different man, confident that he was in a position to retire, which he did shortly thereafter. He and Diane are both retired now and, according to them, loving their new lifestyle.

What more can I say? I love my job.

MAXIMIZING RETIREMENT INCOME STARTS WITH SOCIAL SECURITY

We talked earlier about ways to increase income streams in retirement. Let's look now at some of the options available to do so.

Two common ways to maximize retirement income involve paying less in taxes—that is, keeping more of what you've earned—and getting the most from your Social Security benefits. We're going to spend an entire chapter later on tax strategies, so let's concentrate on Social Security here.

Social Security, the government pension program and social safety net established in 1936 during the Great Depression, is the primary source of retirement income for many retired workers. For some, sadly, it is the only source, which explains in part why we find so many seniors continuing to work because they have to in what should be their retirement years.

Entire books have been written about myriad aspects of Social Security. I personally have a certification to present seminars on the subject, though I'm not doing that here. Still, there are some important things to know when discussing how to get the most from Social Security benefits. This is, after all, a decision that could potentially increase your total Social Security payments by thousands of dollars or more over the course of a lifetime.

1) The full retirement benefit for which you are entitled—based on the involuntary contributions you made to the Social Security Trust

Fund through FICA withholding from your regular paycheck—is due at full retirement age (FRA). For almost all readers of this book, that age is sixty-six or sixty-seven or some period in between[2] (see the following chart). You can track the amount of your full benefit by establishing a personal profile on the Social Security website (www.ssa.gov/myaccount).

Your Full Retirement Age

Year of Birth	Full Retirement Age
1937 or earlier	65
1938	65 and 2 months
1939	65 and 4 months
1940	65 and 6 months
1941	65 and 8 months
1942	65 and 10 months
1943—1954	66
1955	66 and 2 months
1956	66 and 4 months
1957	66 and 6 months
1958	66 and 8 months
1959	66 and 10 months
1960 or later	67

2) A worker who qualifies for benefits, as most readers of this book will, can begin taking them as early as age sixty-two.[3] But as many people know, you will receive a reduced benefit—a reduction averaging about 6 percent a year—for each year you receive benefits before your FRA. Equally important, this reduced benefit is what you will receive for the rest of your life. Your monthly benefit will increase only through cost-of-living adjustments (COLAs) that may or may not be made annually, depending on the rise of inflation.

---

[2] Social Security Administration. 2020. "Full Retirement Age." https://www.ssa.gov/planners/retire/retirechart.html.
[3] A "worker benefit" is different than a disability benefit. Benefits for people with disabilities also are available through Social Security, but this book will deal only with benefits and options available for qualified workers.

Now let's consider more positive news on the subject of when to begin taking benefits.

You will receive an enhanced benefit if you choose to delay taking benefits until after FRA. Your monthly benefit will increase at a rate of 8 percent for every year you delay taking benefits between FRA and age seventy, the point at which these delayed retirement credits end.

Let's plug in some numbers to show the difference in a benefit taken early when compared to one taken at FRA or even later.

The person in this example is scheduled to receive a full monthly lifetime benefit of $2,000 at age sixty-seven, his FRA. If he first begins taking benefits at the earliest possible age (sixty-two), the Social Security Administration says his lifetime monthly benefit will be reduced by 30 percent (an average of 6 percent per year over five years) to $1,400. However, if this same person delays taking Social Security until age seventy, the monthly benefit grows by 24 percent (three years times 8 percent yearly) and becomes a $2,480 per month lifetime benefit.

Consider what those three different benefit levels might mean over the course of a single year.

Delaying Social Security

Early benefit (62)	FRA benefit (67)	Delayed benefit (70)
$1,400 monthly	$2,000 monthly	$2,480 monthly
$16,800 yearly	$24,000 yearly	$29,760 yearly

3) The monthly payment established when first taking benefits—whether at FRA or on an "early" or "delayed" basis—also sets the standard for any spousal or survivor benefit. A spousal benefit is available at the FRA of a spouse who lacks a qualifying work history—a stay-home parent, for instance, who works extremely hard but without employment compensation. This benefit can be up to half of the "working" spouse's benefit. A survivor benefit (which is available as early as age sixty) for a widow or widower is the larger of the two benefits available during the lifetime of a couple. The

Social Security Administration eliminates the smaller of those two benefits following a spouse's death.

When is the best time to begin taking benefits? Only you can answer that highly individualized question. Still, the assistance of a financial advisor with a solid knowledge of Social Security issues as well as a comprehensive view of your broad financial picture can be very helpful in making that decision. But whether or not you seek professional advice, everyone should understand two simple "rules of the game."

Rule 1: The longer you wait to take benefits, the more you will receive in a monthly benefit. Rule 2: The longer you live, the more you will receive in total lifetime benefits.

Now, who knows how long they will live? Answer: Nobody I know.

You can, however, make at least an educated guess based on the longevity history of your family. This is something you know better than the actuaries who establish mortality tables. Your decision on whether to take benefits early, at FRA, or on a delayed basis might well depend on that knowledge.

Other circumstances also come into play.

Maybe you've worked as hard as you can for as long as you can and need an "early retirement" that depends on a Social Security benefit for income. The Social Security Administration tells us that most Americans do take an early benefit, many at age sixty-two. These people do so knowing they will receive a smaller monthly benefit, but they also know they will ultimately receive more checks than do those who wait until a later age to begin taking benefits.

Other people, however, can afford to wait for that later age. Maybe they enjoy full-time employment and don't want to retire until FRA or later. Or, maybe they have enough income in retirement that they don't immediately need Social Security and can afford to let their benefit grow until it stops growing at age seventy. Such people will receive fewer total payments than will those who take benefits earlier, but they will receive a larger benefit each month.

Here is where the issue of longevity enters the picture.

There is a "break-even" point somewhere around age seventy-nine or eighty, at which the total amount of Social Security benefits paid to persons taking "early" benefits, FRA benefits, or "enhanced" benefits becomes equal (see the following chart). Those taking early benefits come out ahead if they don't live to this break-even point. But those living beyond age eighty who delayed taking benefits until FRA or later come out the winner in the total benefits derby.

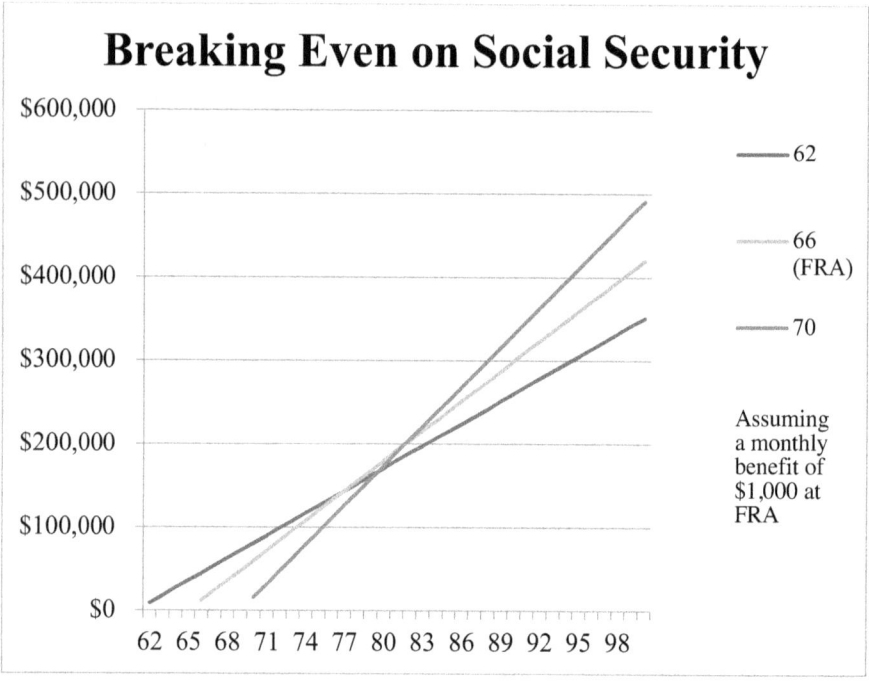

Source: Finance.yahoo.com

Which option is right for you?

By using software that examines your entire financial picture as well as your family longevity, a financial advisor can help you make a more informed choice for this decision that can affect the rest of your life.

TAPPING THE RETIREMENT BUCKETS; WHERE DO I PULL FROM FIRST?

Scenario: Paul and Paula were beginning to think they might go through life without grandchildren. Their son and daughter remained unmarried well into their thirties and expressed little interest in changing that.

Then one day, about a year before Paul's planned retirement date, daughter Amanda decided she was ready for matrimony, and she's not talking about a simple civil ceremony. Paul and Paula, who thought they had an income plan that would get them through retirement, suddenly have to deal with an expensive upcoming wedding.

From which of their retirement accounts will they take the money to pay for a wedding reception—sit-down dinner, open bar, DJ—for 250 people?

Deciding which of your retirement assets will be tapped to fill an income gap is a major decision most people face in retirement.

As noted earlier, many people we see have a variety of such assets. The years leading up to or early in retirement are the time to assemble all these pieces and decide which will be used, and when, to produce essential retirement income when necessary.

In making this decision, you should consider drawing assets in the most tax-efficient way possible from three different income buckets: taxable, tax-deferred, and tax-free. Let's look at each of them.

☐ **Taxable.** These are accounts funded with after-tax money upon which you are currently paying taxes as they grow in value. Examples of assets commonly found in the taxable bucket are savings accounts, money market accounts, and CDs, as well as stocks, bonds, and mutual funds in a brokerage account.

☐ **Tax-deferred.** Some of the most common retirement plans—the 401(k), 403(b), IRA, SEP, SIMPLE, 414(h), TSP, and 457(b)—are tax-deferred accounts, also known as "qualified" accounts. These are accounts created with pre-tax contributions, money upon which you've yet to pay taxes. These accounts are accruing value on a tax-deferred basis, but they are also accruing an additional tax burden that grows in conjunction with the account value. A time is coming, at age seventy-two (for those who were not seventy-and-one-half before January 1, 2020), when you will be required to withdraw money from these accounts and pay taxes on all amounts withdrawn (more on required minimum distributions in our tax planning chapter).

☐ **Tax-free.** The Roth IRA is the most common example of a tax-free account. These accounts have been funded with money upon which you've already paid taxes, and this money grows on a tax-free basis. But unlike tax-deferred accounts, money withdrawn from this bucket incurs no additional taxes, provided certain conditions are met.[4] Beyond that, money in a Roth IRA is not subject to RMDs and can be passed on to heirs who can take distributions without taxes. The same cannot be said of loved ones who inherit tax-deferred accounts and the tax bill that comes with them.

Back to our original question: From which of these tax buckets will you first take additional retirement income when necessary?

Conventional wisdom often suggests that income should first be taken from the taxable bucket. The reasoning? Since you are already paying taxes on these accounts, you can take income from them with only capital gains considerations. Meanwhile, your tax-deferred and tax-free accounts continue to grow. You might even be able to take a little more risk, if your risk tolerance and risk capacity allows it, with the money in qualified accounts that you won't draw from until later in life (we'll discuss risk tolerance and risk capacity in the next chapter on investment planning).

The tax-deferred bucket becomes the second option. But any money taken from these accounts will produce an immediate income tax bill, so the idea is to let these accounts continue to grow in a more tax-advantageous way than the assets in the taxable bucket.

---

[4] Among the conditions under which distributions from a Roth IRA can be taken tax-free: the recipient must be at least 59 ½ years old; the funds must have been in the Roth IRA for at least five years. A tax-free distribution also can be taken at any time by a person with a permanent disability.

The tax-free bucket is one that ideally should be allowed to grow until some point in the future when it becomes absolutely necessary to take income—possibly for health care matters or long-term care. In the upcoming tax-planning chapter, I will detail some ideas on building up our tax-free bucket by converting assets from the tax-deferred accounts.

Why do I suggest this pecking order? Well, would you rather have your accounts that are currently growing with a tax burden continue to grow and create an even larger tax burden? Or, would you prefer to see your accounts that are growing either tax-deferred or tax-free continue to compound without immediately adding to your taxes?

Keep in mind that these "rules" for taking income from the three tax buckets always have exceptions depending on a person's individual situation. There may be random years, for instance, when it can be advantageous to draw from tax-free resources (normally the No. 3 option) as a means of reducing a larger-than-usual tax burden.

Example: Let's say you need to withdraw $25,000 from retirement assets for a new car, or to replace your home's HVAC system or, like Paul and Paula, to pay for a daughter's wedding. Taking even part of this withdrawal from the tax-deferred bucket increases taxable income and has the potential not only to bump you into a higher tax bracket, but also might increase any tax you owe on Social Security benefits. (We'll discuss Social Security taxes in more detail in the tax planning chapter.)

Here is a case where you might take at least some of what you need in a tax-free distribution from a Roth IRA in order to reduce the tax impact brought about by any big-ticket need for additional income. We can help you determine which tax bucket may be appropriate for your special situation.

HOW MUCH MIGHT I TAKE FROM EACH ACCOUNT?

So now you've decided from which of your retirement assets you will take additional income when necessary. The next question: How much can we take annually from these assets without draining them completely?

The 4 percent rule is something of a financial services industry standard you may have heard of. It says, in essence, that a person can withdraw up to 4 percent from all retirement assets in the first year, then adjust that initial amount by 3 percent each following year to account for inflation. Using this strategy, the theory says, a person has a high probability of making whatever assets they have available for a thirty-year period. The theory is that traditional growth in stock and bond values will at least partially offset the outflow of assets taken as income.

Economic conditions have changed, however, since the 4 percent rule was first introduced in 1994 after a study of market returns over a seventy-five-year period.

With the low-interest rates that followed the Great Recession of late 2007 through early 2009, many professionals suggest a reduction of the 4 percent rule. According to an article in *U.S. News & World Report*, a more up-to-date annual withdrawal is closer to 2 to 3 percent.[5]

Consider the consequences for a retired couple with, say, $400,000 in retirement assets at age sixty-six. Under the 4 percent rule, our couple might expect to withdraw $16,000 a year (before adjustments for inflation) to supplement Social Security and other fixed income. A 2.8 percent withdrawal rate, however, would give our couple only $11,200 annually. Clearly, developing alternative income streams—ones that don't rely on investments dependent on the performance of

---

[5] Barbara Friedberg. *U.S. News & World Report.* June 6, 2018. "Why the 4 Percent Withdrawal Rate Is Obsolete."
https://money.usnews.com/investing/investing-101/articles/2018-06-06/why-the-4-percent-withdrawal-rate-is-obsolete

the stock and bond markets—is worth exploring in the current low-interest climate.

ALTERNATIVE INCOME STREAMS; THE ROLE OF ANNUITIES

An annuity is a contract between the annuitant (that's you) and an insurance company. The annuitant makes a payment (a premium) to an insurance company that, in turn, promises to make regular income payments that over time could exceed the amount of premium paid. Some annuity contracts with lifetime income riders—an option that may have an additional cost—even promise payments for the life of an annuitant and/or a spouse. The promise to make payments is backed by the claims-paying ability of the insurance company issuing the contract, much as the ability to make lifelong Social Security payments is backed by the good faith and credit of the U.S. government.

Annuities are not for everyone. But for people looking for alternative sources for sustainable income streams, annuities are a consideration worth making as part of a well-rounded retirement income plan. Let's take a brief look at four basic types of annuities.

- **Fixed annuity.** These offer a fixed interest rate that is typically higher than the rate you might get on a bank product.[6]
- **Immediate annuity.** Unlike a fixed annuity that begins payments only after an accumulation period, an immediate annuity begins income payments either right away or within a short period of time. The annuitant makes a decision at purchase as to how long the insurance company will make income payments, which have

---

[6] Fixed annuities are long term insurance contacts and there is a surrender charge imposed generally during the first five to seven years that you own the annuity contract. Withdrawals prior to age fifty-nine-and-one-half may result in a 10 percent IRS tax penalty, in addition to any ordinary income tax. Any guarantees of the annuity are backed by the financial strength of the underlying insurance company.

the potential to be more than the premium paid because of interest generated over time.

- **Variable annuity (VA).** The contract value of a VA rises and falls daily depending on the market performance of the "sub accounts" the annuitant chooses as investment options, and you can lose money since your money is subject to the market.[7]
- **Fixed index annuity (FIA).** Though not directly invested in the market, the FIA offers the potential for growth through credited interest generated by a rise in whatever market index the contract is linked to. The annuity value is locked in each year on the annuity's anniversary date and cannot be lost to future market drops. Conversely, should the index level fall below the reset value in any given contract year, the contract value remains at its previous level. The contract, in effect, has a floor of $0 in losses, although the cost of any additional riders purchased will continue to be deducted every policy anniversary. This means that, in a worst-case scenario—such as when the S&P 500 fell by more than 38 percent in 2008, then experienced a similar free fall during February and March of 2020—the value of an FIA doesn't lose a dime due to the market. Because FIAs are insurance products that offer guarantees to your money, they also have limits on how much interest you can earn, however, and the interest you earn will generally not equal the full gains of the market index.[8]

---

[7] *Consider the investment objectives, risks, charges, and expenses carefully before investing in variable annuities. The prospectus, which contains this and other information about the variable annuity contract and the underlying investment options, can be obtained from the insurance company or your financial professional. Be sure to read the prospectus carefully before deciding whether to invest.* The investment return and principal value of the variable annuity investment options are not guaranteed. Variable annuity subaccounts fluctuate with changes in market conditions. The principal may be worth more or less than the original amount invested when the annuity is surrendered.

[8] Indexed annuities are insurance contracts that, depending on the contract, may offer a guaranteed annual interest rate and some participation growth, if any, of a stock market index. Such contracts have substantial variation in terms, costs of guarantees and features and may cap participation or returns in significant ways.

The FIA's potential to 1) offer guaranteed income through 2) index-based interest coupled with 3) a protection against loss of principal due to market volatility makes this an attractive choice for many consumers to provide added stability to an income plan.

We will discuss our retirement investment approach further in the following chapter.

One final note on annuities. Provisions of the SECURE Act that took effect on January 1, 2020, allowed for the first time the inclusion of annuities as part of a 401(k) plan. This presents an option that could work well for some people. My personal opinion, however, is that a person interested in an annuity should also consider the options available in the open market and not limit themselves to the often-limited options available within a company's 401(k) plan.

ADJUST FOR INFLATION AND PLAN FOR GROWTH

Inflation will inevitably cut into the buying power of your retirement dollars, which means you also need some growth in your accounts to offset this effect.

We call inflation "inevitable" because, well, when have you known prices on goods and services to go down and stay down? Some of our clients have still vivid memories of when gasoline cost well under $1. On the other hand, most of our visitors also remember when gas was pushing $4 a gallon not that long ago.

Inflation typically has one of the biggest, if not *the* biggest, erosive effect on our retirement savings, ranking just ahead of taxes and health care costs. Numerous longevity studies tell us a retired person at age sixty-six today might well expect to live twenty to thirty years

---

Any guarantees offered are backed by the financial strength of the insurance company. Surrender charges apply if not held to the end of the term. Withdrawals are taxed as ordinary income and, if taken prior to fifty-nine-and-one-half, a 10 percent federal tax penalty. Investors are cautioned to carefully review an indexed annuity for its features, costs, risks, and how the variables are calculated.

in retirement, so you have to account for higher costs whenever you re-evaluate your income plan.

The inflation rate in 2019, 1.71 percent, a figure that inexplicably does not include increases in gasoline and groceries—because who spends money on gasoline and groceries?[9]—was well below the 3.3 percent historical rise over the past century. But even that relatively modest rate of inflation tells us that today's prices have the potential to double in twenty years. This prospect of rising costs has to be countered with retirement asset growth that can at least match (and preferably exceed) the rate of inflation.

Growth in our invested assets is typically a goal in our working years, but in retirement, income is king. Growth is never far from the throne, though, which brings us to our discussion of investment planning.

---

[9] Sarcasm intended.

CHAPTER FOUR

Investment Planning: Know Your Limits in Retirement

*S*cenario: *Tim and Sue love to travel. This Nebraska couple might take a few trips each year to Kansas City to catch a Royals or Chiefs game and enjoy some barbecue. Most winters find them in Florida catching some rays on a Gulf beach.*

Another place they enjoy visiting on occasion is Las Vegas. They don't go there every year, but they've visited Nevada maybe a dozen times over the past twenty years. They go for the shows more than The Strip, and are more interested in seeing, say, Cirque du Soleil than they are in visiting Circus Circus. But, as a popular expression, "when in Rome," suggests, they figure they might as well see Caesar's Palace, which is Tim's light-hearted way of saying he likes to play blackjack every once in a while.

Neither is what anyone would call a big gambler. Before each trip they designate a set amount of money they can afford to lose. When that money is gone, they leave. Should they be up a bit after a couple hours, they also know to walk away with what Tim laughingly calls "my return on investment."

They play with money from their self-imposed retirement entertainment budget. This is what they consider "disposable income," money not needed for routine living expenses. This is money other people might allocate to season tickets for Cornhusker football, Broadway shows on tour in Omaha, annual hunting trips in Canada, or fishing trips on the lakes of northern Minnesota. Some people spend their retirement entertainment dollars on winter excursions in the desert climate of Arizona. Tim and Sue like the desert, too, but they prefer the Sahara.

Tim and Sue's approach to at-risk money serves as an illustration, of sorts, of our philosophy on investment planning, the second component of our Pathway for Retirement™.

That approach, put as simply as possible, is this: As people approach or are or actually in retirement, they simply cannot afford to gamble with money they cannot afford to lose. Having said that, we also believe there is an essential place in retirement planning for growth in our retirement assets, and that this growth may involve some degree of risk. The adage we've heard all our lives—"No risk, no reward"—is as true in retirement as it was in our working years.

The key to taking risk in retirement, however, involves knowing you can do so without using money needed for essential living expenses. At Shunkwiler Financial, we believe it is **only after** establishing a detailed income plan—one that lets a person or couple know their retirement income needs will be met by predictable, sustainable income that can last a lifetime with inflation factored in—that we can even begin to think about the growth of our investment assets.

This growth is important for future income, money we likely will need later in life when health care expenses become an even bigger consideration. But growth doesn't come without some element of risk. And that risk, at whatever level you choose to take, can be easier to live with when we are not dependent on our at-risk investments for retirement income.

Which brings us back to Tim and Sue. They've done their income planning. They know they have sustainable income to meet their regular living expenses. They also know they have some "disposable income" for entertainment, recreation, travel, and the other lifestyle dreams for their retirement years. Good for them. The money they spend in Vegas is money set aside for the enjoyment and entertainment they dreamed of experiencing in retirement. It is not money designated for routine living expenses. This is a big part of what retirement planning is all about.

RISK TOLERANCE IN RETIREMENT

Taking investment risk in retirement is a somewhat different version of what we knew throughout our working years when most of us made regular contributions to our retirement assets, often through a 401(k) or some other retirement plan.

Taking on higher risk in the hope of reaping a higher reward was something we often did willingly as younger savers and investors. We could invest somewhat aggressively (if we chose to do so), knowing our investments had ample time to recover any value lost to inevitable market downturns, corrections, and even recessions. "Don't worry, the market comes back," is a historically accurate adage that helped us keep the faith in our investment strategy even when market conditions such as those induced by the COVID-19 virus panic challenged that belief.

People nearing or in retirement, however, often can't afford a long-term outlook when they face the short-term prospect of having to sell retirement assets to create essential income.

"Risk tolerance" is a concept we likely first heard shortly after beginning any initial meeting with an investment counselor. Risk tolerance is a guess, an estimate of how aggressive one wants to be with investments. It asks, basically, what kind of investment loss would you be willing to take in hopes of reaching a higher gain?

It's not uncommon to hear younger investors, people willing and able to take a long-term view of an investment strategy, say confidently that they could tolerate a 10, 15, even 20 percent or higher loss in an investment portfolio. They wouldn't feel especially good about that kind of loss, but they wouldn't lose sleep, either.

But our risk tolerance typically changes as we get older. The investments we make then should reflect this.

It's often been said that the ten most important years of our financial life are the five before retirement and the five just after.

These are the years when we really don't want something bad to happen as it did in 2008 and again in 2020. The 38 percent loss in the 2008 market (as measured by the S&P 500 index) becomes more than a mathematical measuring stick when we must rely on declining-value assets for retirement income.[10]

Let's explore this in real numbers.

Let's say you were sixty-four in 2008. Perhaps you'd already retired, or were planning to do so soon. You've got $400,000 in retirement assets. You've done some basic income planning and estimate that you can take 4 percent of those assets annually, or $16,000, and fill the income gap between your anticipated yearly expenses and what you receive from Social Security and any other regular income.

In 2008, however, that nest egg loses 30 percent and declines in total value to around $280,000. You fully expect that value to rebound over time, but for right here and now you still need $16,000 yearly for supplemental income. For a while, at least, you will have to take 5.7 percent of $280,000 to fill your $16,000 income gap.

Beyond that, in a down market such as the Great Recession of 2008 or the virus panic of 2020, you suddenly have to sell more shares of your assets (because of the reduced price of each share) to generate the same level of income. Moreover, after doing this you will have fewer remaining shares that have the opportunity to grow when the market rebounds (as it did in 2009 when it was up more than 23 percent).

Given the scenario of 2008, or even earlier in 2002 when the market fell 23.7 percent, a person looking at retirement might quickly sense their retirement nest egg disappearing faster than initially

---

[10] Indices are unmanaged and investors cannot invest directly in an index. Unless otherwise noted, performance of indices do not account for any fees, commissions or other expenses that would be incurred. Returns do not include reinvested dividends. The Standard & Poor's 500 (S&P 500) is an unmanaged group of securities considered to be representative of the stock market in general. It is a market value weighted index with each stock's weight in the index proportionate to its market value.

planned. If you don't think that idea doesn't keep some people awake at night, think again.

This is where risk tolerance becomes more than theoretical. Now we are talking about the concept of "***risk capacity***," which can be defined as an actual amount of money—a very real dollar figure—that you simply cannot afford to lose. Put another way, losing more than this amount would force you to change your lifestyle. You would have to live off less, go out less, maybe even put off doing a lot of things you had hoped to do.

You might even have to go back to work or work a lot longer than you planned before retiring.

What you had back in 2008 when the market crashed was time. Now, ten-plus years removed from that period, you are within five years of retirement and you probably don't have the time to recover if the market were to crash again as it did twelve years later.

Are you willing to take that kind of risk with your investments this close to, or already into, retirement? I highly doubt it. This is why knowing one's risk capacity is a crucial part of making retirement investment decisions.

JUST HOW "SAFE" ARE YOU?

Many people follow a basic investment strategy as we grow older. The common strategy in our later years is to reduce risk by lowering exposure to the more volatile stock market investments such as stocks and mutual funds. The 60/40 split between stocks and bonds we might have held at age forty often flips at age sixty to a 40/60 split that favors income-producing bonds and other more conservative investments.

But many people nearing retirement don't realize the actual risk level of their investment portfolio.

We see many clients on a first-time basis who tell us they are conservatively invested in preparation for retirement. Yet when we take a closer look at their assets using a software program—we employ one from a company called Riskalyze—that measures the risk level of an investment portfolio, many are startled to learn they are actually at a greater level of risk than they imagined.[11] Some may be perfectly comfortable at that level. Others, not so much. For this later group, some portfolio adjustments may be in order.

But let's go back to an important point here that bears repeating. That is, ***a person really can't determine their retirement investment comfort level until first developing an income plan that covers multiple years of retirement.***

A properly developed income plan, one that assures you a lifetime stream of predicable income designed to sustain the retirement lifestyle of your choice, can also estimate how much of your assets might be invested for future growth.

Having this knowledge can also help a person be a smarter investor in retirement. Investing money that you don't absolutely need for essential income allows one the opportunity to follow the "buy low, sell high" advice we've heard throughout our lives. Knowing you can sell assets to generate income when you *want to* as opposed to when you *have to* gives one the option to avoid selling at the worst possible times during market downturns. Knowledge of your regular income flow also helps establish the risk level you are willing to take with the money you feel free to invest.

---

[11] The projections or other information generated by Riskalyze regarding the likelihood of various investment outcomes are hypothetical in nature, do not reflect actual investment results, and are not guarantees of future results. These figures may exclude commissions, sales charges or fees that, if included, would have had a negative effect on the annual returns. Investing is subject to risk and loss of principal. There is no assurance or certainty that any investment strategy will be successful in meeting its objectives.
The Six Month 95 Percent Probability Range is calculated from the standard deviation of the portfolio (via covariance matrix), and represents a hypothetical statistical probability, but there is no guarantee any investments would perform within the range. There is a 5 percent probability of greater losses. The underlying data is updated regularly, and the results may vary with each use and over time.

VOLATILITY CONTROL

Scenario: Mike and Cathy are close friends with Dick and Jane. Occasionally over the course of a backyard barbecue, when the two men finally stop discussing the current state of the Nebraska football team, the topic of investments comes up.

"Our advisor was just showing us how well we've been doing these past couple years since the recession," Dick said one evening in 2019. "We've had double-digit gains in seven of the last ten years since then. Man, we were up 32 and 22 percent in two of those years."

"Glad to hear it," Mike replied. "Cathy and I aren't getting anything close to that. We got maybe three 10 percent increases in that time."

"Maybe it's time to talk to my guy."

When he does talk to "his guy," Mike may find he's doing better than he imagined, and perhaps even better than Dick.

Consider the two following charts that depict the hypothetical accounts of both couples.

Chart A is the investment portfolio of Dick and Jane. It is invested in an S&P 500 index fund that began in 2000 with a $1 million balance. The couple has been taking 4 percent annual withdrawals from their original balance, or $40,000 in income each year, since then.

The chart shows some very significant gains that Dick likes to talk about. But there also are some significant losses, too, such as during the "dot-com bubble burst" from 2000 to 2002 and again during the worst full year of the Great Recession (2008). The account has recovered nicely since then with multiple years of double-digit gains including a 26 percent rise in 2009, a 32 percent bump in 2013, and a nearly 22 percent jump in 2017.

At the end of a nineteen-year period, after total withdrawals of $760,000 during those years, this account still had a balance of roughly $730,000. Their average gain over the period is 6.32 percent.

Chart A: Performance of hypothetical fund based on historical returns of S&P 500 index

Year	Portfolio 1	Beg Bal	Earnings	Withdrawal	End Bal
2000	-9.06%	$1,000,000	-$90,600	-$40,000	$869,400
2001	-12.02%	$869,400	-$104,501	-$40,000	$724,898
2002	-22.15%	$724,898	-$160,564	-$40,000	$524,333
2003	28.50%	$524,333	$149,434	-$40,000	$633,768
2004	10.74%	$633,768	$68,066	-$40,000	$661,835
2005	4.77%	$661,834	$31,569	-$40,000	$653,404
2006	15.64%	$653,404	$102,192	-$40,000	$715,597
2007	5.39%	$715,596	$38,570	-$40,000	$714,167
2008	-37.02%	$714,167	-$264,384	-$40,000	$409,783
2009	26.49%	$409,782	$108,551	-$40,000	$478,334
2010	14.91%	$478,334	$71,319	-$40,000	$509,654
2011	1.97%	$509,653	$10,040	-$40,000	$479,694
2012	15.82%	$479,693	$75,887	-$40,000	$515,581
2013	32.18%	$515,581	$165,914	-$40,000	$641,496
2014	13.51%	$641,495	$86,666	-$40,000	$688,162
2015	1.25%	$688,161	$8,602	-$40,000	$656,764
2016	11.82%	$656,763	$77,629	-$40,000	$694,393
2017	21.79%	$694,393	$151,308	-$40,000	$805,701
2018	-4.43%	$805,701	-$35,692	-$40,000	$730,009
Average	6.32%				
Std Dev	17.61%				

Hypothetical example(s) are for illustrative purposes only and are not intended to represent the past or future performance of any specific investment.

Now check out Chart B, which projects the returns on Mike and Cathy's portfolio.

This is a much more conservative portfolio whose components are a fixed index annuity (FIA) along with an actively managed account of stocks, mutual funds, and some bonds. This portfolio, like that of Dick and Jane, also started in 2000 with a beginning balance of $1 million. (Aren't coincidences wonderful?) Mike and Cathy also are taking 4 percent annual withdrawals from their initial balance, or $40,000 each year. Their account gains from year-to-year aren't anywhere near as spectacular as those of Dick and Jane, but their losses in the down years are also nowhere near as steep.

At the end of the same nineteen-year period, their account balance (again, after $760,000 in withdrawals) is $1,581,608—more than twice the value of Dick and Jane's portfolio even though their average return is about 0.46 percentage points less. The key difference in the two accounts is in the downside, as Mike and Cathy lost much less in the down years of the market.

Chart B: Projected return of managed portfolio that includes FIA

Year	Portfolio 2	Beg Bal	Earnings	Withdrawal	End Bal
2000	3.83%	$1,000,000	$38,300	-$40,000	$998,300
2001	-0.03%	$998,300	-$299	-$40,000	$958,001
2002	0.18%	$958,000	$1,724	-$40,000	$919,725
2003	18.57%	$919,724	$170,792	-$40,000	$1,050,518
2004	9.23%	$1,050,517	$96,962	-$40,000	$1,107,481
2005	5.50%	$1,107,480	$60,911	-$40,000	$1,128,392
2006	10.70%	$1,128,392	$120,737	-$40,000	$1,209,130
2007	4.08%	$1,209,130	$49,332	-$40,000	$1,218,463
2008	-1.16%	$1,218,462	-$14,134	-$40,000	$1,164,328
2009	10.45%	$1,164,328	$121,672	-$40,000	$1,246,001
2010	8.20%	$1,246,000	$102,172	-$40,000	$1,308,173
2011	5.06%	$1,308,172	$66,193	-$40,000	$1,334,366
2012	8.07%	$1,334,366	$107,683	-$40,000	$1,402,050
2013	10.01%	$1,402,049	$140,345	-$40,000	$1,502,395
2014	7.81%	$1,502,394	$117,337	-$40,000	$1,579,732
2015	-1.74%	$1,579,731	-$27,487	-$40,000	$1,512,244
2016	3.74%	$1,512,244	$56,557	-$40,000	$1,528,802
2017	9.78%	$1,528,802	$149,516	-$40,000	$1,638,319
2018	-1.02%	$1,638,319	-$16,710	-$40,000	$1,581,608
Average	5.86%				
Std Dev	5.26%				

Hypothetical example(s) are for illustrative purposes only and are not intended to represent the past or future performance of any specific investment.

What makes the difference? Simply put, Mike and Cathy have some level of volatility control built into their portfolio.

Check out the standard deviations—a measure of volatility—on each account. Dick and Jane have a standard deviation of 17.6 percent compared to a 5.26 percent volatility measure for Mike and Cathy. Dick and Jane from 2008 through 2013 experienced a plunge of 37 percent and an upward rush of 32 percent. That's a wild swing of 69 percentage points in their account value over a six-year period—a lot of volatility by any account. Mike and Cathy, on the other hand, experienced a 1.16 percent decline in their worst year (2008) with two 10 percent gains as their best times. That's an eighteen-point swing that was well within their range of risk tolerance.

While Dick and Jane's account experiences the full rollercoaster ride of the market—rising to dizzying new heights with occasional scream-inducing-plunges—Mike and Cathy's portfolio is more of a gentle spin on the merry-go-round. The FIA that is a part of their portfolio limits their participation in market gains, but it also features a guarantee of no loss of invested principal during market downturns. Mike and Cathy consequently don't experience the full rush of the ride to the top during market "go-go" times, but they also aren't holding on for dear life during the market's inevitable "oh-no" free falls.

Which ride are you willing to take in retirement?

That choice is up to each individual investor depending on what is right for their particular financial situation. But knowing what you can afford to "gamble" in regard to your retirement investments remains a key. It is only after determining that level that you can choose how to play your chips.

Let's look now at how we might do just that.

YOUR ASSETS MAY BE AT RISK; PREPARE TO PLAY DEFENSE

If you haven't already guessed by now, I'm a big fan of the University of Nebraska football program. As a lifelong fan, I vividly remember the glory days of the Black Shirts, the name given to the Cornhuskers defense that once played a huge role in the years the program contended for, and won, national championships.

I still believe in a strong defense today in my role as a financial advisor. That's because playing defense can be especially important in the years both before and during retirement when our assets are subject to various risks. Among these risks:

- Our own need for income to supplement what we receive from Social Security and other regular income streams. Another part of this risk: Our desire for additional income to enjoy some of the "frills" we've looked forward to experiencing in retirement.
- Our Uncle Sam. He'll come calling soon to get tax payments on those tax-deferred investments you made for years in a 401(k) or IRA. What, you thought he forgot about you?
- Our own bodies. No one stays *Forever Young*, despite Bob Dylan's hopeful sentiment to the contrary. Our bodies break down over time, and though advances in medical treatments have helped us live longer on average, such medical care comes at a cost that only increases as we get older and require more care.

Having said that, let's note there is still a need to play offense in retirement. That is, to have growth potential in the retirement assets that are subject to risk.

The difference in retirement—to once again employ a football analogy—is that you don't want your offense to put your defense in a bad position.

How might we go about doing this?

THERE ARE INVESTMENT TOOLS TO CHECK THE BOXES

One strategy I like suggests our retirement investments should address three particular concerns: income, protection, and growth. This is easier said than done, however, as few investments can accomplish all three goals.

Dividend-producing stocks, for instance, have the potential to produce income and growth but offer little in the way of guarantees. Bonds can generate income with a lower level of volatility than equities, but they offer little potential for growth. Bank CDs are about as guaranteed as an investment can get, but their potential for both income and growth are extremely limited in today's low-interest climate.

So, what's a retirement investor to do when seeking growth as well as income and some degree of relative protection?

There are a number of financial products that offer the potential for both growth and income while protecting your principal from loss in value due to market volatility. Let's look briefly at two such products.

THE FIXED INDEX ANNUITY (FIA)

A properly structured FIA as described in detail in the previous chapter offers the potential for growth through credited interest each year that is tied to an increase in whatever market index the insurance contract tracks. The annuitant receives a designated percentage of any interest created by the index hike, subject to limits set by the company.

An FIA also has a contractually obligated promise against loss of principal due to market performance, based on the financial strength and claims-paying ability of the issuing company. This is a risk taken on by the insurance company that issues the contract.

Finally, an FIA also is capable of producing income through systematic payments that are based on the contract's account value. This contract value is a number that has the potential to last for many years even as income withdrawals are taken.

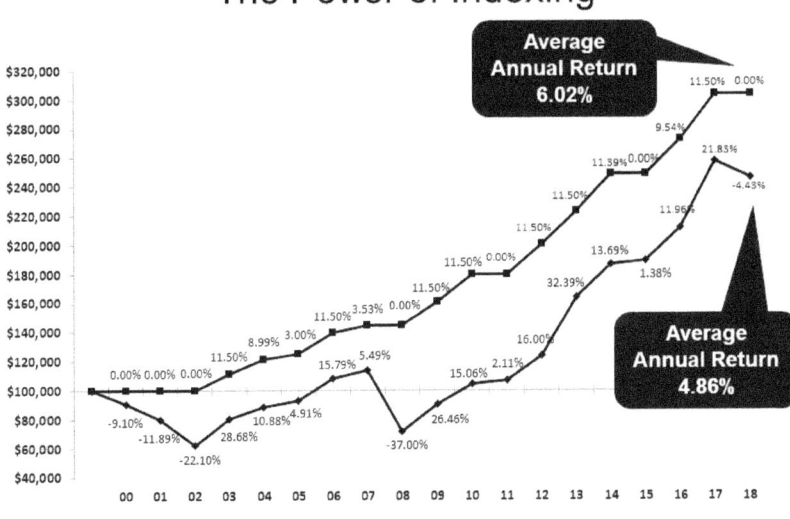

Source: Yahoo Finance GSPC Historical Prices, accessed 01/20/2019

This historical performance of the S&P 500® is not intended as an indication of its future performance and is not guaranteed. This graph is only intended to demonstrate how the S&P 500, excluding dividends, would be impacted in an indexed universal life insurance product with a hypothetical growth cap of 11.5 percent and floor of 0 percent. It is not a prediction on how any IUL product might have operated had it existed over the period depicted above. The actual historical growth of an IUL product existing over the period depicted above may have been higher or lower than assumed, and likely would have fluctuated subject to product guarantees. This graph does not reflect the impact of life insurance policy charges or investment account fees, so actual comparative values may vary from this chart.

While the preceding chart is used to demonstrate potential indexed growth in an IUL, it also illustrates how a fixed index annuity functions with capped growth, an annual reset, and a protection against loss of principal due to market volatility. The capped growth in an FIA is typically not as great as the 11.5 percent cap used in the IUL illustrated above.

INDEXED UNIVERSAL LIFE INSURANCE (IUL)

The role of permanent life insurance in retirement is often overlooked by seniors. Sure, some will say, we needed life insurance when we were younger to guarantee income protection for our young family in the event of our untimely demise. But, life insurance in retirement? At this age? What's the point?

"The point" is that there are permanent life policies that offer not only a death benefit for your heirs, but also the potential for tax-free growth of the policy's cash value and income—in addition to protection against loss of principal due to market declines. As with all life insurance, the death benefit will be paid tax-free to your named beneficiaries, part of the legacy portion of our Pathway to Retirement™ plan.

Let's briefly examine the basic functions of fixed indexed universal life insurance (IUL), a product that also has a place in our tax planning and health care strategies.[12]

Like all insurance contracts, an IUL begins with a premium paid either on a one-time or recurring basis. This premium is the basis of the policy's cash value that has the potential to grow through the power of indexing—that is, credited interest that is based on a rise in the market index to which the policy is linked. The policy is credited with a designated percentage of such interest, if any, subject to limits set by the company. As is the case with a fixed index annuity, when interest is credited, the policy's cash value is reset at a new level that cannot be reduced by future market losses. The insurance company assumes all risk in protecting against loss.

Beyond that, the policy also is capable of producing income while the insured is still alive. This income is taken in the form of distributions that are tax-free if properly structured. These withdrawals will reduce the policy's death benefit and cash values and could cause the policy to lapse or require additional premium payments, so you need to manage your policy carefully over the long

---

[12] Indexed universal life insurance is an insurance contract that, depending on the contract, may offer a guaranteed annual interest rate and some indexed interest, if any, of a stock market index. Such contracts have substantial variation in terms, costs of guarantees, and features, and may cap participation or returns in significant ways. Any guarantees offered are backed by the financial strength of the insurance company, not an outside entity. Consumers are cautioned to carefully review an indexed universal life insurance for its features, costs, risks, and how the variables are calculated.

term to ensure it performs as you intended. This gives the insured the opportunity to use at least part of the policy's death benefit while still alive. The IUL thus provides a potential alternative source of retirement income when needed. As with all life insurance, it involves fees, charges and limitations, and you may need to qualify for it through the underwriting process.

Both the FIA and IUL also offer alternative sources of funding that can be used for long-term care—something we'll discuss in greater detail in the upcoming health care chapter.

These options are not for everyone, but you might consider discussing them with us to determine whether they are appropriate for your retirement portfolio.

CHAPTER FIVE

Tax Planning: How Much Will Be Yours to Keep?

There are many reasons for Shunkwiler Financial's emphasis on tax planning, the third leg of our Pathway for Retirement™ plan and the most technical aspect.

A couple of the most prominent reasons for our emphasis on tax planning:

- One, we believe that, in retirement, what matters more than what you have saved is how much of that you get to keep after taxes.
- Two, that we now have lower tax brackets in place that allow us to employ some time-sensitive tax-saving strategies that may not be available much longer.

Let's look at that last item first.

The Tax Cut and Jobs Act of 2017 effectively reduced marginal tax rates across the board. These lower tax brackets are scheduled to expire at the end of 2025 unless they are revised amid the ever-shifting winds of American politics. The key aspect of this temporary tax restructuring is that most of the tax rates for each bracket have been lowered. As you'll see in the following chart, what was a 15 percent tax rate in one bracket is now 12, the 25 percent bracket is now 22, and the 28 percent bracket has been lowered to 24, as illustrated in the following chart.[13]

---

[13] Amir El-Sibaie. TaxFoundation.org. November 10, 2016. "2018 Tax Brackets." https://taxfoundation.org/2018-tax-brackets/

Single-Filer Brackets

2017		2018	
Tax rate	Taxable income over:	Tax rate	Taxable income over:
10%	$0	10%	$0
15%	$9,325	12%	$9,525
25%	$37,950	22%	$38,700
28%	$91,900	24%	$82,500
33%	$191,650	32%	$157,500
35%	$416,700	35%	$200,000
39.6%	$418,400	37%	$500,000

Married Filing Jointly Brackets

2017		2018	
Tax rate	Taxable income over:	Tax rate	Taxable income over:
10%	$0	10%	$0
15%	$18,650	12%	$19,050
25%	$75,900	22%	$77,400
28%	$153,100	24%	$165,000
33%	$233,350	32%	$315,000
35%	$416,700	35%	$400,000
39.6%	$470,700	37%	$600,000

The bottom line, for a while at least, is that we have the opportunity to take action to help our tax situation. To do that, however, requires action sooner rather than later. We will look in more detail later in this chapter at some tax strategies that take advantage of these lower brackets over the next several years, but let's first look at how taxes in retirement can be greatly different from those we knew in our working years.

THE RETIREMENT TAX PICTURE

All your working life you've more than likely grumbled about taxes. That isn't going to change in retirement.

There will be differences, however.

For one thing, a tax break many readers of this book received throughout our working years—whether we knew it or not—is coming to an end.

That's right, we got a tax break when we made voluntary contributions to our 401(k) or IRA or any other "defined-contribution" retirement plan.

We likely didn't think a lot back then about those pre-tax contributions that seemed more like ordinary payroll deductions than tax-deferred investments in our future. What mattered more in those years was that a portion of our income was not being taxed, or not *yet* anyway. What's not to like about that?

Sure, we always knew in the back of our minds that we would pay tax on that money someday later in life. But retirement seemed decades down the road then, so we likely paid little attention to the long-range consequences of tax-deferred income. We also may have been told our tax bracket would likely be reduced in retirement after we stopped receiving a regular paycheck and our annual income was lower.

It seemed like a pretty good deal at the time, right?

But now you are nearing or are well into retirement, and the tax picture takes on a new look. For many people, their retirement income might not be greatly reduced after all, and neither is their tax bracket. This only makes sense. They worked hard to generate a retirement income that at least comes close to what they knew while working. Good for them; one shouldn't plan for a reduced standard of living in retirement.

Beyond that, however, those taxes you legally deferred over all those working years are now about to become due. What, you thought Uncle Sam just forgot about them?

Many people in retirement find that, once they finally have to start paying taxes on all that tax-deferred income, their tax picture looks pretty much the same, ***if not higher***, than what they knew in the working world.

This is why strategies to legally reduce our tax payments in retirement become extra important. When our regular paychecks stop coming in, it's time to work on keeping as much of our money in our pocket as possible.

REQUIRED MINIMUM DISTRIBUTIONS: THE BILL COMES DUE

The time to pay the piper—a.k.a., Uncle Sam—for all those tax-deferred investments made throughout our working years comes at either age seventy-and-one-half or seventy-two. This is when we are required to begin taking fully taxable required minimum distributions (RMDs) from our IRAs, 401(k)s, and other tax-deferred accounts, also known as "qualified" accounts.[14]

The difference between the two RMD ages is a result of the SECURE Act (Setting Every Community Up for Retirement Enhancement) that took effect January 1, 2020. The act delayed what the IRS calls the "required beginning age" for RMDs to seventy-two for people who had not reached age seventy-and-one-half prior to January 1, 2020.

Many readers of this book understand the basic concept of RMDs, but let's explore a few critical points here at the start.

An RMD is an amount that *must* be withdrawn each year from a person's qualified accounts upon reaching their required beginning age. This amount is based on the total value of all qualified assets (such as IRAs) at the end of the previous year. That total is then divided by an IRS life expectancy factor (see the following chart) with the result being that year's RMD amount. The life expectancy factor lowers each additional year, which means the RMD is likely to increase each year as we age.

---

[14] An RMD exception exists for people who continue to work past the required beginning age and are still participating in a company-sponsored 401(k). Such people do not have to begin taking RMDs until after they stop working and participating in the 401(k).

IRS UNIFORM LIFETIME TABLE
(As of January 1, 2020)

Age	Distribution Period	Age	Distribution Period
70	27.4	93	9.6
71	26.5	94	9.1
72	25.6	95	8.6
73	24.7	96	8.1
74	23.8	97	7.6
75	22.9	98	7.1
76	22.0	99	6.7
77	21.2	100	6.3
78	20.3	101	5.9
79	19.5	102	5.5
80	18.7	103	5.2
81	17.9	104	4.9
82	17.1	105	4.5
83	16.3	106	4.2
84	15.5	107	3.9
85	14.8	108	3.7
86	14.1	109	3.4
87	13.4	110	3.1
88	12.7	111	2.9
89	12.0	112	2.6
90	11.4	113	2.4
91	10.8	114	2.1
92	10.2	115+	1.9

Example: Let's say you have three IRA accounts that total $450,000. The largest of them is a $400,000 IRA created by a rollover of the company-sponsored 401(k) you built over your working years.

Let's also say you turned seventy-and-one-half before January 1, 2020. By April 1 of the year after you reached seventy-and-one-half, you had to take a mandatory, fully taxable distribution based on the $450,000 total in all three qualified accounts.[15] You *do not* have to

---

[15] IRS rules stipulate that a person is deemed to be seventy-and-one-half six months after reaching their seventieth birthday. Example: A person who turned

take a distribution from *each* account, but you must withdraw the RMD number determined by the total value of all three IRAs. Your first required minimum distribution would be $16,423, a figure determined by dividing $450,000 by 27.4, the "life expectancy factor" for a person at age seventy as determined by the IRS Uniform Lifetime Table listed above.[16]

A person who would turn seventy-and-one-half on or after January 1, 2020 would take their first RMD at age seventy-two. Using the same $450,000 accounts total as in the example above, this person's first RMD would be $17,578—$450,000 divided by 25.6, the life expectancy factor at age seventy-two. The RMD in each of the above two examples is the total amount you must withdraw from your qualified accounts, and you will be taxed at your regular tax rate on every cent of that amount.

A couple of other important points here.

Uncle Sam is determined to get the tax owed on our tax-deferred money. The IRS consequently will impose *a 50 percent penalty* on any annual required distribution amount not taken.

---

seventy in the first half of 2019 (that is, on or before June 30, 2019) is deemed to have reached the qualifying age for RMDs in 2019. Such a person must take an RMD by no later than April 1, 2020, based on the total value of all qualified accounts at the end of 2018.

The April 1 RMD deadline applies to only the first RMD taken after reaching the qualifying age. All subsequent distributions must be taken by December 31 and will be based on the total value of all qualified accounts as of December 31 of the preceding year. Source: "Required Minimum Distributions (RMD)." www.irs.gov/publications

A person born in the second half of 2019 (on or after July 1, 2019) is deemed to have turned seventy-and-one-half after January 1, 2020—the date upon which new RMD rules of the SECURE Act took effect. Such a person would not have to take an initial RMD until the year in which they turn seventy-two. The deadline for taking a first RMD remains the same, April 1 of the year after reaching age seventy-two. The distribution deadline for all subsequent years is December 31. Source: "Important RMD Information," Security Benefit, February 2020.

[16] Separate life expectancy tables exist for people who inherit an IRA (the Single Life Expectancy Table) as well as for IRA owners whose spouses are more than ten younger and are the sole beneficiaries of the owner's IRA (the Joint Life and Last Survivor Expectancy table). Source: IRS Publication 590-B, "Distributions from Individual Retirement Arrangements." www.irs.gov/retirement-plans

Moreover, somebody is eventually going to pay these taxes someday. Uncle Sam would prefer to get this tax payment from the original account owner during their lifetime, but he will collect the tax owed on any remaining balance of a qualified account from anyone who inherits that account. We will discuss inherited IRAs in more detail in our chapter on legacy planning.

Let's also note here that when two spouses have their own qualified accounts, a separate RMD is required of each spouse. A couple cannot take a single RMD based on their combined "number."

DIFFERENT RULES ON IRAS, 401(K)S

One final note, one not commonly known even by those familiar with required minimum distributions.

The rules governing RMDs on an IRA differ slightly from those on defined contribution accounts such as the 401(k), 403(b), 457(b), SEP, SIMPLE, TSP, or others.

The distribution levels are the same, but IRS rules ***require*** a person after reaching their required beginning age to take an annual distribution from a 401(k) or other plans listed above. A person owning multiple IRAs, however, is ***not required*** to take a distribution from each account so long as they somehow satisfy their total RMD number based on the value of all accounts. The IRS doesn't care how you meet your RMD number on IRA accounts, but the rules are different on employer-sponsored plans.

This is one reason why I might recommend clients to roll over their 401(k) or other defined-contribution accounts into a personal IRA after leaving the company that offered the 401(k) (the rollover itself is done without a tax obligation, though taxes will still be owed on all tax-deferred money in the new IRA whenever funds are withdrawn). Not only can you have more control over how the money in that rollover IRA is invested—remember, investment choices in a company-sponsored 401(k) are usually limited to only those offered by the plan—but you also have more control over how and when you will take your required distributions.

I also suggest that clients consolidate all their qualified accounts under one financial umbrella and use one advisor to "be the quarterback" for the purpose of more accurately determining their annual RMD. Let's explain that.

Every financial services company that administers a qualified account is required to inform the account owner of their annual RMD. But if you have qualified accounts scattered among several different companies, keeping track of all the RMD numbers can become difficult and increases the likelihood of mistakes when you have to take your total RMD. The IRS has provisions that allow you to correct such mistakes and avoid a penalty, but the best way to avoid such a situation is to correctly meet your RMD number in the first place. Getting that number from one source instead of several is a good way to avoid an IRS penalty that can be substantial.

A COMMON EFFECT OF RMDS: SOCIAL SECURITY TAXES

The annual RMD, whether a person needs it for income or not, is considered ordinary income and is taxed accordingly in whatever tax bracket you reside. This added income has the potential to affect our tax picture in two ways.

1) It could bump you into a higher tax bracket.
2) It can affect the taxes you might need to pay on your Social Security benefits.

Let's look at that last situation first.

Not everyone pays taxes on Social Security. Benefits were not taxed from the program's inception in 1935 until 1983, when Congress first established income thresholds beyond which up to 50 percent of a person or couple's benefits could be taxed. In 1993, Congress went a step further by establishing a higher income threshold over which up to 85 percent of a benefit could be taxed.[17]

---

[17] The 50 and 85 percent figures do not mean that Social Security benefits are

SOCIAL SECURITY TAXATION CHART

If you are ___ and your provisional income is ___ ...		... you will pay taxes on ___ of your Social Security benefits.
Single, Widow(er), Head of Household	*Married Filing Jointly*	
<$25,000	<$32,000	0%
$25,000-$34,000	$32,000-$44,000	50%
$34,000<	$44,000<	85%

The key to whether Social Security benefits are taxed is "provisional income," which is different from ordinary income.

Also known as "modified adjusted gross income (MAGI)," provisional income consists of all the components that go into calculating adjusted gross income on IRS Form 1040. Among these elements are 1) wages; 2) self-employment income; 3) taxable interest, dividends, and capital gains; 4) taxable income from IRAs, pensions, and annuities; and 5) income received from rentals, alimony, royalties, and trusts, along with other miscellaneous income items.

But other factors also go into determining MAGI. The biggest of these is one-half of the total Social Security benefits received in a tax year by an individual filer or a couple filing jointly. Tax-exempt interest (such as that created by municipal bonds) also is a part of provisional income.

A quick glance at the preceding chart shows it doesn't take much provisional income to exceed the 50 percent level—$25,000 for an individual filer, and $32,000 for a married couple—that was established in 1983 and which has not been adjusted for inflation since then. The 85 percent level (which hasn't been adjusted since its inception in 1993)—$34,001 for an individual and $44,001 for a couple—also isn't especially high in terms of today's dollars.

---

taxed at rates of 50 or 85 percent. Rather, these figures represent the percentage of a person's benefits that can be taxed at that person's normal tax rate.

These levels were deemed to be a tax on "the rich" when they were first established in 1983. So, if you are an individual with provisional income of $25,000 or a couple earning $32,000 or more, the federal government apparently considers you "rich." Congratulations, how does that feel?

Clearly, additional ordinary income created by RMDs—income that may or may not be needed or wanted to meet our regular expenses—is something that should be considered when a person takes a big-view look at their retirement tax picture. Here is where strategies designed to limit the hidden effects of RMDs can come into play.

DRAINING THE TAX-DEFERRED BUCKET: ROTH CONVERSIONS

As noted, we can't completely avoid paying taxes on our tax-deferred assets. Someone is eventually going to pay that bill, and if it's not you, it will be your loved ones or anyone else who inherits your qualified assets and the tax bill that goes with them.

There are, however, strategies that can spread out this tax obligation and provide some leeway to take distributions (and pay the resulting taxes) at more tax-advantageous times of our choosing. I believe the tax structure in place today allows us the opportunity to take advantage of these strategies.

To more fully explain that, please consider this question:

Knowing that you or an heir must someday pay taxes on all tax-deferred assets, would you rather pay the bill at the 15, 25, or 28 percent rates scheduled to go back into effect in 2026 (unless they are extended), or the 12, 22, and 24 percent rates available from 2018 through 2025?

The best known of these tax strategies, the Roth IRA conversion, gives us the opportunity to reduce or eliminate the tax-deferred bucket, an option wielding even more impact in the tax-friendly climate of today. Moreover, it gives us the opportunity to build up our tax-free bucket with assets we or our heirs can access without the burden of future taxes.

The Roth IRA conversion strategy has been around for years, and many readers are likely familiar with the concept. Even so, let's briefly review some basics.

The Roth IRA conversion involves moving assets from the tax-deferred bucket—such as a traditional IRA or 401(k)—into a tax-free bucket. Moving money out of tax-deferred accounts means paying those unpaid taxes. But draining the tax-deferred bucket, particularly over a period of years, has the ultimate effect of lowering (or completely eliminating) future RMDs.

By moving the after-tax balance of their IRA to a Roth IRA, a person has the opportunity to continue growing these assets tax-free. Over time, that continued growth has the potential to help offset the taxes paid on the IRA withdrawal. Future withdrawals from the Roth IRA will be tax-free, assuming you are older than fifty-nine-and-one-half and the account has been open for at least five years. Inheritors of a Roth IRA will not pay taxes on that money. Moreover, a Roth IRA has no taxable RMDs[18] and does not factor into the equation for determining provisional income on Social Security. When considering a Roth IRA conversion, however, it is important that you have funds to pay the taxes due upon conversion instead of taking this money out of your IRA account in order to realize the greatest benefit from the conversion.

Strategic timing has always been a factor in choosing whether and/or when to make a Roth IRA conversion. As taxes are due on any amounts being converted, a person thinking about a conversion should consider the most tax-advantageous time to do so.

These times could come in the first several years of retirement when our income and taxes might be somewhat reduced. These are the years before RMDs kick in, with their potential to move us into a higher tax bracket. Other opportunities might come in any year when

---

[18] Inheritors of a Roth IRA are required to take annual distributions that are based on the age of the inheritor. Such distributions are made on a tax-free basis to the inheritor.

we have high medical deductions or losses in business income that reduce our tax obligation. An unexpected job loss, or the opportunity to take an early-retirement buyout—not an uncommon situation for older Americans in today's job climate—might also present an opportunity to withdraw more money from our qualified accounts.

The reduced tax brackets created by Congress in 2017 and implemented in 2018 give many people another tax-friendly time to turn tax-deferred money into tax-free money. Remember the former 15 percent tax bracket has now been reduced to 12 percent. The 25 percent bracket is now 22, and the 28 percent bracket is now 24.

How much longer will these reduced tax brackets be in effect? They are scheduled to expire at the end of 2025, but one can only guess what might happen before or after that time. The point is that these lower brackets are here today, and they present an opportunity worth considering.

Moreover, the new RMD required beginning age (seventy-two) established by the SECURE Act for persons who turn seventy-and-one-half on or after January 1, 2020, now gives such people an additional year and a half to make Roth conversions. That's an additional eighteen months over which one can spread out inevitable tax payments in today's more tax-friendly income brackets.

The decision on whether or when to do a Roth IRA conversion is one that should be considered with professional help. My company, which routinely works with an accountant during this decision-making process, stands ready to help you decide if this tax strategy is right for you.

A COMPARISON: RMDS VS. ROTH IRA CONVERSION

Whatever choice you make regarding your tax-deferred assets is strictly a personal one. Some people prefer dealing with their RMDs, and the resulting taxes that come with them, each year as they come due. Others opt to drain what they can from their tax-deferred bucket before RMD time, choosing to pay taxes now instead of later.

I wouldn't begin to suggest what might be best for you without taking a detailed look at your current investment and tax situation. Even so, a comparative look at the tax savings of a Roth IRA conversion versus the potential taxes incurred from taking regular RMDs on a traditional IRA might be helpful here.

For the purpose of this hypothetical illustration, we will assume that Tim is age sixty-five and that his RMD required beginning age was seventy-and-one-half. He has $400,000 in tax-deferred assets in a traditional IRA that he established soon after retiring through a rollover of his 401(k). We will further assume that this IRA has an annual net growth rate of 3.5 percent. Tim and his wife, Sue, had an adjusted gross income of between $78,000 and $82,000 during the last years of Tim's working career. They were in a 25 percent tax bracket through 2017, but are now in a 22 percent bracket after the changes of the Tax Cut and Jobs Act were implemented in 2018.

After hearing about Roth IRA conversions in a discussion with their financial professional and becoming aware that they could do such a conversion at a lower tax rate, Tim and Sue set out to see if it would be more tax-friendly to take annual RMDs or to gradually convert all of Tim's IRA into a Roth IRA.

Let's look at their two examples. To see the chart that summarizes the numbers, you can skip ahead a few pages, but following is the detailed breakdown of this scenario.

In **Example A**, Tim must begin taking RMDs at age seventy-and-one-half and pay the tax on each distribution. He will then reinvest the after-tax remainder—as he and Sue believe they will not immediately need the RMD for income—in market-based investments earning a conservatively estimated average annual return of a net 3.5 percent. Tim will continue paying taxes on the growth of these investments as interest, dividends, and capital gains are realized.

Example B shows Tim's plan to completely convert his tax-deferred IRA into a tax-free Roth IRA.

Over a five-year period beginning at age sixty-five, Tim will convert $80,000 each year into his Roth. This $80,000, his tax accountant advised, was a figure Tim and Sue could take annually without being bumped from their new 22 percent bracket into the 24 percent bracket that begins with an adjusted gross income of $165,000 for married couples filing jointly. Tim and Sue elect to pay their tax obligation on the converted money directly from the $80,000 they will withdraw in each of the five years of their plan. Again, as explained a couple of pages earlier, we feel it is most beneficial to pay for the taxes from another account rather than directly from the account (IRA) that you are converting to pay the taxes, however for simplicity in this example we are paying the taxes from the same account.

At the end of the five-year plan, when Tim reaches the required beginning age to take RMDs, he will have paid a total of $88,000 in taxes. (By way of comparison, his tax bill on that same $400,000 conversion would have been $100,000 had he and Sue still been in the 25 percent bracket.) His tax-free Roth IRA will be increased by $312,000 (the after-tax remainder of the $400,000 withdrawn from the IRA), and Tim has no remaining tax-deferred assets requiring an RMD. Moreover, his Roth IRA has the potential to continue growing tax-free.

Let's now look at Tim's hypothetical tax picture at age ninety.

In **Example A**, after twenty years of taking RMDs and paying tax on each amount every year, Tim will have paid some $106,850 in taxes on the required distributions. After twenty years of reinvesting the after-tax remainder of those RMDs at a net 3.5 percent growth rate, he will have paid another $54,515 in taxes on the growth of his taxable investments. If Tim were to pass away at age ninety, he would leave behind an IRA with an approximate $65,861 tax burden to whomever inherits it, presuming those people are in the same tax bracket.

All totaled, during twenty years of taking RMDs from age seventy to ninety, Tim and his heirs might pay out roughly $227,299 in taxes on what once was a $400,000 IRA.

Now let's look at **Example B**.

In converting his IRA to a Roth IRA over a five-year period, Tim paid $88,000 in taxes on the $400,000 he converted. But after doing so, he has a Roth IRA with $0 in future taxes. Tim will pay *no tax* on any money he takes from the Roth, and anyone inheriting his Roth also will incur no taxes.

Bottom line: In the twenty-five years since he first began doing a Roth IRA conversion at age sixty-five, Tim's total tax bill is $88,000. Compare that to his total tax bill after twenty years of taking RMDs—$227,229.[19]

IRA Taxes

Example A Annual RMDS on traditional IRA		Example B Roth IRA conversion	
Projected taxes on RMDs, 70 to 90	$106,850	Taxes on conversions, 66 to 70	$88,000
Taxes on reinvested RMD growth	$54,518	Taxes on Roth growth	$0
Taxes on inherited traditional IRA	$65,861	Taxes on inherited Roth	$0
Total taxes	**$227,229**	**Total taxes**	**$88,000**

Admittedly, the Roth IRA conversion strategy is not for everybody. Many people balk at the idea because of the short-term tax consequences of moving large amounts of money from a tax-deferred

---

[19] These figures are for informational purposes only and are not intended to provide tax, accounting, or investment advice. Be sure to consult qualified professionals about your individual situation. This hypothetical example does not consider every product or feature of tax-deferred accounts or Roth accounts and is for illustrative purposes only. It should not be deemed a representation of past or future results, and is no guarantee of return or future performance. Your tax bracket may be lower or higher in retirement, unlike this hypothetical example. RMD calculation data gathered from © 2019 Stonewood Financial Solutions RMD calculation software based on IRS guidelines and tables, and is hypothetical only. Your actual RMDs are determined by a variety of factors.

to a tax-free bucket. These tax consequences, to say nothing of the impact on taxable income in the years when conversions are done, can be especially dramatic when a conversion is made on a one-time, lump-sum basis. This is why most people making Roth conversions do so with smaller amounts over an extended period of time. Some may not drain all of their tax-deferred bucket, but any reductions they make now are often appreciated later when RMDs enter the picture.

To repeat a point made in Tim's conversion plan: A critical part of a Roth IRA strategy is to convert an amount that does not push you into a higher tax bracket. This is why we like to involve an accountant when considering Roth conversions.

There are other considerations, as well.

One, while the annual amount that can be contributed to a Roth IRA is currently limited—people with earned income can contribute $6,000 annually, and people age fifty or older can contribute up to $7,000 annually—there are no limits on amounts in a Roth IRA conversion.

Two, Roth IRA conversions are often done in the years before RMDs begin, but they are not limited to that time. The difference is, once RMDs begin, you cannot transfer the full amount taken from an IRA directly into a Roth. You can, however, withdraw *more* than the required distribution from an IRA and convert the additional balance into the Roth.

Again, the bottom line on Roth conversions lies in the understanding that tax-deferred assets will incur a tax bill that is going to be paid eventually by somebody, either you or your heirs. The choice is yours on when, and by whom, that bill will be paid. Some parents see the short-term tax hit they take in draining the tax-deferred bucket as a long-term legacy gift to adult children or grandchildren who might someday inherit a Roth IRA without a tax burden.

BE STRATEGIC IN HOW YOU TAKE RMDS

Even if the Roth IRA conversion strategy is not for you, there are still opportunities to be strategic in how you take your required minimum distributions.

As noted earlier in this chapter, one doesn't have to take an RMD from every account in an IRA. True, a person facing RMDs has a number to meet each year, but the IRS doesn't especially care what qualified assets you tap to reach that number.

This presents some strategic opportunities for people with one or more IRAs. A typical IRA likely includes different types of investments—stocks, bonds, mutual funds, etc. Some of these investments will perform better than others every year. We can help you identify the better-performing accounts and potentially take RMDs from them in the most efficient way.

Some people take regular monthly or quarterly distributions, paying the taxes owed through either withholding or estimated quarterly payments. This method can serve to provide a more consistent flow of regular income. Other people prefer to take their RMD in one lump sum, often at the end of the year as the deadline nears for taking an RMD. Others opt to take interest, dividends, and capital gains from their qualified accounts and apply those distributions toward meeting their RMD number.

Keep in mind here that the IRS is more concerned about **when** you pay the taxes than it is with **how** you take the taxable required distributions.

Uncle Sam prefers to collect tax revenue on a steady, "as earned" basis. This is why taxes are withheld from each paycheck during our working years. This is also why an "underpayment penalty" exists for those people who fail to make what the IRS considers timely tax payments throughout the year. The IRS has a tax payment threshold that, if exceeded, could result in an underpayment penalty and a notice that you are required to make quarterly estimated payments.

The prospect of making estimated tax payments can be a new concept for some people in retirement. But these payments often become the "new normal" once we begin receiving income from Social Security, pensions, IRA distributions, and other sources that are relatively new to us. One always has the option to have tax taken from any of these payments, but many people in retirement prefer to get their regular income in its entirety now and worry about taxes later, typically during the tax reporting season each spring.

And then one day the IRS sends a letter advising of an underpayment penalty and the need to begin making estimated tax payments four times a year in April, June, September, and January.

SO, I'VE GOT THIS RMD MONEY; NOW WHAT DO I DO?

Well, just because you must take money from your tax-deferred accounts doesn't mean you have to spend it, though you certainly can if you wish. If you need an RMD for regular income, by all means, use it. If you need extra money for a daughter's wedding or a bathroom remodel, it's there. After all, isn't this the reason we saved and invested all those years?

But what if you don't need your RMD for regular or disposable income, at least not at the present time?

You can always reinvest this money in the growth vehicle of your choice, provided it is not in another qualified retirement account. CDs, stocks, bonds, mutual funds, annuities—the entire field of investment choices is available in a tax-free Roth IRA or a taxable brokerage account.[20] Your level of risk tolerance and capacity should dictate any investment decisions you make here.

---

[20] *Mutual funds are sold by prospectus. Please consider the investment objectives, risks, charges, and expenses carefully before investing in mutual funds. The prospectus, which contains this and other information about the investment company, can be obtained directly from the fund company or your financial professional. Be sure to read the prospectus carefully before deciding whether to invest.*

Certain tax strategies might also come into play, especially for people looking for ways to offset the taxes on RMDs.

The Roth IRA conversion is a leading option. Consider Tim's example. He converted a $400,000 IRA into a Roth with a $312,000 after-tax balance. If he realizes a modest 4 percent annual growth rate in the tax-free Roth, Tim could potentially see his account balance back at $400,000 in six to seven years, although we can't offer any guarantees as to what the market will do in the coming years.

The tax deductions available to those making donations to their church or other charitable organization are another way to partially offset the tax impact of RMDs. Consider, too, other tax-friendly options such as municipal bonds.

One option to consider is using the RMDs to pay premiums on a permanent life insurance policy in which the cash value can potentially be used for tax-free income as well as for assistance in paying for long-term nursing care. Assuming you can qualify medically for coverage, the tax-free death benefit available to beneficiaries is a legacy component of life insurance that we'll discuss in more detail later.

Let's wrap up our discussion of tax planning in retirement by noting that taxes are a known unknown. That is, we know there will always be taxes, but we don't know the rate at which we will pay them. What will the tax rates be after the lower rates established by the Tax Cuts and Jobs Act expire at the end of 2025? No one can say for sure.

What we do know, however, is that a relatively tax-friendly environment is in place today. The opportunity to employ some tax strategies exist here and now, and you owe it to yourself and your loved ones to at least talk about them.

CHAPTER SIX

Health Care Planning: Getting Older Can Be Expensive

It's often said that the only things certain in life are death and taxes, and we'll add here the rising costs of health care.

No matter how hard we work to maintain a healthy lifestyle, our bodies break down over time in the natural process of aging. Dealing with this inevitable decline comes with a cost.

In its 2019 annual Retiree Health Care Cost Estimate, Fidelity Investments estimated that a retired couple at age sixty-five should expect to spend $285,000 in health care expenses over the course of their remaining lifetime.[21] Estimated expenses for a single retiree are $150,000 for women and $135,000 for men.

Fidelity's 2019 estimate for lifetime medical care is $5,000 more than its 2018 estimate, and more than 16 percent higher than its 2015 figure. But cheer up; Fidelity reports the two-year rise in its estimate from 2018 to 2019 is 3.6 percent slower than the rise from 2015 through 2017 (12.2 percent). Does that make you feel better?

Didn't think so.

---

[21] The Fidelity Retiree Health Care Costs Estimate assumes individuals do not have employer-provided retiree health care coverage but do qualify for Medicare. The calculation takes into account cost-sharing provisions (such as deductibles and coinsurance) associated with Medicare Part A and Part B. It also considers Medicare Part D (prescription drug coverage) premiums and out-of-pocket costs, as well as certain services excluded by Medicare. The estimate does not include other health-related expenses such as over-the-counter medications, most dental services, and long-term care. Source: "Health Care Price Check," Fidelity Investments, April 2, 2019.

How much a person or couple might spend on lifetime medical expenses can be skewed considerably if long-term nursing care enters the picture.

In October 2019, the American Council on Aging reported that the Nebraska statewide average "private pay" cost for a shared room in a private nursing facility was $230 a day and $83,950 a year.[22] Don't like the idea of sharing a room? The statewide average for a private room in 2019 was $253 a day—and $92,345 a year. The average costs for nursing home rooms in Lincoln are even higher. The average daily cost for a semi-private room in the state capital is estimated at $236 ($86,140 annually) with a private room estimated at $271 daily and $98,915 annually.

All of the above estimates may be higher or lower for an individual or couple, but the point remains that health care expenses in retirement can quickly eat up a big piece of any retirement nest egg. A person or couple must plan to eventually deal with this kind of expense, which is why health care planning is an essential fourth leg in our Pathway for Retirement™ process.

HOW DOES ONE PAY FOR THESE ADDITIONAL COSTS IN RETIREMENT?

Finding ways to pay for this care is one of the major challenges in retirement planning.

Yes, Medicare will help considerably when we qualify for its benefits at age sixty-five. But as most readers know, Medicare doesn't pay for all medical expenses in retirement. It is the responsibility of each retiree to find ways to pay the difference. We will discuss Medicare and "Medigap" coverage in more detail later in this chapter.

One way to finance your health care is through personal funding. Some people with substantial retirement nest eggs are able to

---

[22] Source: "Nursing Home Costs by State and Region 2019." American Council on Aging, Oct. 24, 2019. https://www.medicaidplanningassistance.org/nursing-home-costs/

designate a large portion of their savings exclusively for future health care expenses. Good for them, but even these people may find it mentally challenging not to use these earmarked funds for other purposes should the need or the desire to "raid" these funds arise.

Another option is Uncle Sam's tax-friendly way to save for future health care needs.

Maintaining a Health Savings Account (HSA) is an option best implemented before age sixty-five, as HSA contributions are not allowed after one qualifies for Medicare.

Prior to then, however, a couple or family can contribute up to $7,100 a year (the limit for 2020), or an individual up to $3,550 annually, of pre-tax money into a fund that has the potential to realize tax-free growth.[23] Distributions can be taken from an HSA either before or even after age sixty-five on a tax-free basis for any certified medical need.

There are other alternative ways of funding retirement health care needs that we'll explore later in this chapter. But let's first look at some brief basics of the primary way most Americans pay for health care in retirement.

THE BASICS OF MEDICARE

Medicare, established in 1965, is the government's health care plan for seniors.

"Traditional" Medicare consists of four parts. People already receiving Social Security benefits are automatically enrolled in Parts A and B three months before reaching age sixty-five. Coverage starts at the first of the month in which a person reaches age sixty-five.

---

[23] To be eligible to make HSA contributions, an individual or family must be enrolled in a "high deductible" health plan. The IRS in 2020 defined a high deductible plan as one having a minimum annual deductible of $1,400 for individual coverage and $2,800 for family coverage. Persons aged fifty-five and older can make "catch-up contributions" of an additional $1,000 to an HSA. Source: "IRS announces 2020 Health Savings Accounts limits." May 29, 2019, *Forbes* magazine, www.forbes.com

Persons not yet receiving Social Security have to register to begin receiving Parts A and B.

PART A

Also known as "hospital insurance," Medicare Part A provides in-patient coverage that begins only after a doctor-ordered admission.[24] Outpatient surgery and emergency room treatments are not covered by Part A. Care in a skilled nursing facility following a hospital admission is completely covered for a period of twenty days, and patients are responsible for co-insurance costs ($170.50 daily in 2020) for a stay of between twenty-one and one hundred days. Hospice care also is covered when certain conditions are met. Some home health services also are covered.

Part A premiums are paid through the Medicare tax that is part of regular Social Security withholding. People who paid Medicare taxes over a period of forty quarters—the ten-year work history required to qualify for full Social Security benefits—pay no additional Part A premiums.[25] People with less than forty quarters of Medicare taxes pay a monthly premium of between $252 and $458 (figures for 2020) to receive Part A coverage.

PART B

Also called "medical coverage," Medicare Part B covers physician services, outpatient care, preventative services, medical supplies, and equipment, as well as some diagnostic procedures such as laboratory costs and imaging exams. Part B also covers durable medical equipment (such as blood sugar monitors, hospital beds, canes and

---

[24] Part A coverage requires hospital in-patient deductible and co-insurance payments. The deductible that must be paid by the patient is $1,408 (the 2020 figure) per benefit period. The per-day coinsurance rate for 2020 is $352 for a hospital stay or between sixty-one and ninety days. There is no coinsurance charge for the first sixty days of hospitalization. Source: "What Medicare covers: Part A coverage—hospital care." www.medicare.gov/what-medicare-covers/

[25] A person does not have to work forty *consecutive* quarters to qualify for either Social Security or Medicare Part A coverage.

crutches, oxygen equipment, etc.), as well as a portion of ambulance services and mental health care.

Part B coverage is not free health care. It comes with a monthly premium that is based on income (see the following chart). Persons receiving Social Security benefits have this premium deducted from their monthly benefit payment. Persons participating in Part B but not yet taking Social Security pay the premium out of pocket.

Medicare Part B 2020 Premiums

Individual Taxable Income	Joint Taxable Income	Monthly Premium
<$87,000	<$174,000	$144.60
$87,000 - $109,000	$174,000 - $218,000	$202.40
$109,000 - $136,000	$218,000 - $272,000	$289.20
$136,000 - $163,000	$272,000 - $326,000	$376.00
$163,000 - $500,000	$326,000 - $750,000	$462.70
$500,000<	$750,000<	$491.50

(Data from Medicare.gov)

Part B coverage is optional, but there is a lifetime penalty for people who add this coverage after declining to take it when first eligible. The penalty is a 10 percent surcharge added to the monthly premium for every year a person was eligible for Part B coverage but opted not to participate.

A notable exception to this penalty is made for people beyond age sixty-five who have health insurance that provides coverage comparable to that of Medicare. Such coverage is typically provided by an employer-sponsored plan available to a worker and often a spouse. These people pay no penalty if they enroll in Part B immediately after leaving their job and losing their employer-provided health insurance plan.

PART C

More commonly known as Medicare Advantage, Part C is a program the Centers for Medicare and Medicaid Services describe as an all-in-one alternative to traditional Medicare. Advantage plans are offered by private insurance companies who contract with Medicare to provide all benefits included in Parts A and B. These insurance companies are in turn compensated by Medicare for services covered. Most Advantage plans also include Part D prescription drug coverage as well as offer limited coverage for vision, hearing, and dental work—services not covered by traditional Medicare.

Medicare Advantage plans can be purchased for little or even no monthly premium.[26] The trade-off for the lower premium is that covered services are available primarily through a network of doctors, hospitals and other medical providers that have contracts with each insurance company. Medicare Advantage operates in much the same way as health maintenance organization (HMO) and preferred provider organization (PPO) health insurance plans that employ deductibles and coinsurance payments. But unlike traditional Medicare, most Advantage programs have an annual out-of-pocket limit to the costs incurred by participants.

PART D

Medicare Part D is optional prescription drug coverage. This is additional coverage that is not included in "traditional" Medicare but is provided through insurance companies working with Medicare. Depending on the monthly premium paid for a Part D plan, an insured person might pay little to no cost for generic prescription drugs, though higher costs are typically associated with brand-name drugs. As a cost-saving measure, some Part D providers designate the retail or home-delivery pharmacies that participate in their plan.

As is the case with people declining Part B coverage without being covered by an alternate plan, there could be a lifetime premium penalty imposed on those who add Part D coverage years after becoming eligible.

---

[26] Medicare Advantage participants continue to pay regular Part B premiums in addition to any monthly Advantage premium. Source: "Costs for Medicare Advantage Plans." www.medicare.gov/our-medicare-costs

MEDIGAP COVERAGE (AKA MEDICARE SUPPLEMENT INSURANCE): PAYING FOR WHAT MEDICARE DOESN'T

Medicare can be a blessing for people who typically face increasing health care issues in their senior years. But Medicare was never intended to cover all of our health care expenses in retirement.

As most people learn upon approaching retirement, Part B covers only 80 percent of Medicare-approved charges for physician services and other medically necessary outpatient treatments. Even Part A hospital coverage comes with an in-patient deductible ($1,408 in 2020) for each benefit period, as well as coinsurance costs for a hospital stay exceeding sixty days.[27]

A patient's 20 percent share of Part B expenses may not seem daunting at first glance. But consider the impact that 20 percent share might have on a person needing extended treatment for cancer, a disease the AARP says can devastate wealth as well as health.

Citing studies by the Fred Hutchinson Cancer Center in Seattle, the AARP in 2018 estimated the average cost for cancer treatment in the United States—including surgeries, chemotherapy, radiation, physician services, post-care medications—at around $150,000.[28] A Medicare patient's 20 percent of such a tab is $30,000.

Imagine how such an expense might impact a retirement nest egg of, say, $200,000? Now imagine the impact if that cancer treatment exceeds the national average, which many do. Imagine also the high health care costs in dealing with other chronic diseases such as stroke, heart disease, kidney disease, or dementia.

This is where Medicare supplemental insurance, also known as Medigap coverage, enters the picture.

---

[27] Medicare defines a "benefit period" as the time beginning on the first day of admission to a hospital or skilled nursing facility (SNF). The period ends sixty days after you have been dismissed from the hospital or SNF. Source: "The Benefit Period." www.medicareinteractive.org/get-answers

[28] Peter Moore. *AARP The Magazine*. June 18, 2018. "The High Cost of Cancer Treatment."

Medigap coverage is offered by private insurance companies to cover some or all of what traditional Medicare doesn't. The extent of the Medigap coverage depends on the plan you choose and the monthly premium you pay. This supplemental coverage is generally accepted by any medical provider that accepts Medicare patients. Beyond that, Medigap coverage also may pay some of the deductibles and coinsurance costs of traditional Medicare. Medigap coverage will not, however, pay for medical services not covered by traditional Medicare.

Note that while Medicare Advantage (Part C) is not considered Medigap supplemental coverage, both serve much the same purpose.

While we can do only so much to protect ourselves from devastating diseases—we can exercise regularly, maintain a healthy diet, reduce stress, refrain from smoking, etc.—there are things we can do to protect our retirement assets from the significant expenses associated with disease. Medigap supplemental insurance helps do this by paying for some or even all of the medical charges not covered by traditional Medicare. Advantage plans serve a similar cost-control function through an annual limit on out-of-pocket expenses, a feature not available through traditional Medicare or Medigap coverage.

Both Medigap coverage and Medicare Advantage plans have their own unique features. The choice of whether to pursue coverage that complements traditional Medicare, as well as choosing which option to employ, is entirely up to you.

Keep in mind that any initial choice one makes is not chiseled in stone. Seniors have the option to change their Medigap or Advantage plans on a yearly basis during Open Enrollment Periods from October 15 through December 7 each year. These periods are most noted for the deluge of mail and TV ads that promote different options, but they also allow us to make changes when necessary.

Example: Let's say you know you have hip replacement surgery looming in the upcoming year. During the Open Enrollment Period, you might consider upgrading your Medigap plan from one that pays part of what Medicare doesn't to one that pays much or all of the patient share. Or, the specialist you've seen regularly for years moves out of the provider network available in your Advantage plan. You might well find that physician in another Advantage network, or you might switch to a supplemental plan that covers his or her charges.

Decisions regarding your initial Medicare and supplemental options, as well as any changes you might make later, can be complicated and are often made more easily with the help of a Medicare advisor. Our company routinely works with several such specialists and stands ready to make recommendations to our clients.

LONG-TERM CARE: A WHOLE NEW WORLD OF EXPENSES

As noted earlier in this chapter, the need for sustained long-term care (LTC) adds another costly dimension to retirement health care costs.

In its 2019 "Cost of Care Survey," Genworth Financial—an insurance company that began looking at long-term care costs in 2004—estimated that seven of every ten Americans now at age sixty-five could require some kind of long-term care in their lifetime.[29] That care could come in any number of ways, from in-home care to assisted living to years spent in a in a skilled nursing facility. The following breakdown shows the national median cost of the various LTC services as determined by the Genworth survey.

MONTHLY COST 2019

In-home care
- Homemaker Services $4,290
- Homemaker Health Aide $4,385

Community and assisted living
- Adult Day Care $1,625
- Assisted Living Facility (Private, One Bedroom) $4,051

---

[29] Genworth Financial. 2019. "Cost of Care Survey 2019." www.genworth.com/agingandyou

Nursing home care
- Semi-Private Room $7,513
- Private Room $8,517

Medicare, unfortunately, provides little help in financing LTC—a fact that surprises some people.

They fail to realize, perhaps, that Medicare is designed to cover "acute" medical care—treatment for people expected to recover from an injury or illness—as opposed to providing "custodial" care for people who need long-term assistance in performing normal activities of daily living. Medicare will pay for twenty days of post-hospital rehabilitation care in a skilled nursing facility, and has coinsurance coverage for up to one hundred days. But the average stay in a skilled nursing facility for a person dealing with dementia (or any other condition that makes permanent care necessary) is anywhere from two to two-and-a-half years *on average*.

How does a retired person, or more likely that person's loved ones, go about paying for such costly care over that length of time?

Long-term care insurance exists for this very purpose, but it is not as widely promoted today as it once was. There are a variety of reasons for this.

It can be expensive, for one thing, with annual premiums of anywhere from $3,600 to $10,000. The wide cost range is based on a multitude of factors, among them the health history of the insured, the extent of the care that will be covered, and the company issuing the policy.

Moreover, long-term care coverage isn't available to everyone; an insurance company must first determine whether you are medically qualified to be underwritten for such coverage. Beyond that, fewer companies today are writing LTC policies now that more and more people need them. And some companies that once were major players in this market are no longer in business.

ALTERNATIVE FOR FUNDING LONG-TERM CARE

Fortunately, some insurance-backed alternatives have been developed to help address the need for traditional long-term care insurance.

One such product is permanent life insurance. Many policies today offer an option—not available in all states—to use a significant portion of the policy's death benefit, sometimes as much as 50 percent, for long-term care. This option generally becomes available when the insured cannot perform two of the six activities of daily living—eating, dressing, bathing, transferring, toileting, and maintaining continence.

Any use of the death benefit reduces the value of that benefit to heirs, but the idea of using life insurance benefits while still alive is appealing to many people, especially those facing potential budget-busting long-term care costs.

Not everyone can be underwritten for life insurance coverage—any number of health conditions or even an unfortunate family health history could present a disqualification. Yet, even people whose health disqualifies them from long-term care insurance or permanent life insurance protection still have an insurance-backed option for alternative health care financing: annuity contract riders.

Without getting too deep into the inner workings of an annuity, let's note that a fixed index annuity (FIA) with an income or long-term care rider can provide lifetime income as well as some benefits that can be used for long-term care.

Here is an example of how that might work:

Ted purchased an FIA with $220,000 from a rollover of his 401(k) and purchased an additional guaranteed income rider. After ten years of growth, his income rider value had grown to $430,000. The insurance company issuing the contract determines Ted's guaranteed lifetime income payment on that amount to be $21,500 annually (5 percent of $430,000). Should Ted need assistance in paying LTC costs, he could access up to $43,000 annually (double the amount of the annual income payment) under the provisions of that annuity contract for a defined period (usually three to five years).

As you can see, there are many options for planning to fund your future needs, both in terms of regular health care and long-term care. To repeat a point mentioned earlier, understanding your Medicare and other health insurance options in retirement can be confusing. Our office works routinely with specialists in this area and stands ready to help connect clients with their services if necessary.

CHAPTER SEVEN

Legacy Planning:
Leaving a Part of You That Lives on

It's a comment made as a joke more often than not. You sometimes hear it when a younger family member says something that irritates a senior parent.

"Well," Mom might say with a (sometimes) feigned look of indignation, "I guess this means you're out of the will now."

It's one thing to joke about losing an inheritance, but legacy planning is hardly a laughing matter. For the concept of "legacy" involves much more than "who gets Mom's money."

Legacy is how you will be remembered when you're gone, and this should involve more than what you leave to others in terms of dollars and cents. Legacy should be about lasting memories of a life well lived, and you don't need your name on a public building, a charitable foundation, or a highway marker to achieve that. It's an honor, of course, to have your name forever attached to a gift to your church, a service project you funded, or a scholarship you endowed. But legacy can just as easily be memories of the lifelong impact you made on a grandchild's life, perhaps through the financial help you provided for their college education. It might be the memories you leave of experiences you shared with kids or grandkids, perhaps from a dream trip you shared together.

Legacy planning, the final component of our Pathway for Retirement™ plan, involves preparation as much as giving. The way you organize your affairs can also be a part of how you are remembered. It may not seem like much now, but those organizational skills will likely be very much appreciated by your loved ones someday during what might be one of the worst times of their lives. When they are still mourning your passing, you don't want them having to pillage your desk drawers and file cabinets looking for essential documents such as your will and life insurance policies.

To be sure, you will likely have financial assets to be passed on to loved ones (you probably wouldn't be reading this chapter if you didn't have such assets). A challenge in legacy and estate planning is to pass these assets in the most organized and tax-efficient manner possible. Moreover, you also want to be sure that the assets you spent your lifetime acquiring will be passed to the loved ones or charitable organizations you want to receive them.

Legacy and estate planning also involve preparing for a time when you may need someone to make decisions on your behalf should you be incapable of making your intentions known due to physical or mental incapacitation.

We'll talk later in this chapter about some legal aspects of estate planning, especially as it involves the probate process. But as I'm not a lawyer—though I work frequently with attorneys who specialize in estate planning—let's first talk about one estate planning option that can easily make your legacy gift available to loved ones or any other cause that is important to you.

LIFE INSURANCE: A WAY TO LEAVE TAX-FREE MONEY TO YOUR HEIRS

Life insurance is one of the most efficient ways I know to make sure that you leave something for a spouse and other people you love in a tax-friendly way. Life insurance is a way of leveraging a smaller amount of money (the premium you pay) into a larger death benefit that will be paid tax-free to the beneficiaries you chose. This money is paid out without the involvement of the probate court system.

We've already discussed in a previous chapter some other "living benefits" of permanent life insurance. The ability to take income from some policies is one such benefit. The ability of some policies to serve as a funding source for long-term care is another. Using these options can help protect some of the wealth you hope to leave for others. And while using "living benefits" of life insurance sometimes reduces the death benefit of the policy, you know that whatever remains of that benefit will be passed on tax-free to the people or charities of your choosing.

As a final note on life insurance, let's point out that a tax-free death benefit generated by an insurance policy can often produce more money for a beneficiary than that available from a taxable inheritance.

THE INHERITED IRA: A TAX BILL WAITING TO BE PAID

Some people don't give much thought to what happens to the remaining balance in an IRA or 401(k) that might be inherited. In failing to consider this aspect of legacy planning, they overlook the tax consequences of what should be a gift to those you love.

As we discussed back in our tax planning chapter, any money in a "qualified account" such as an IRA or 401(k) comes with a tax liability whenever funds are withdrawn, whether on a voluntary or mandatory basis. Someone is going to pay that tax bill someday. If taxes are not paid by the original IRA owner, the obligation falls to the inheritors of the account who in effect receive a reduced legacy gift.

The IRS rules that govern inherited IRAs are complicated and often require the help of a tax professional to navigate. I won't even try to explain all of them here as IRS publication 590-B (Distributions from IRAs) is nearly a hundred pages long. But stripped down to its basics, the IRS gives a non-spousal inheritor of a traditional IRA several options.

1) Take a lump-sum distribution that incurs a tax bill on the entire amount received. This tax obligation must be paid in the tax year the distribution is taken.

2) Non-spousal beneficiaries who inherited an IRA prior to January 1, 2020, must either liquidate the inherited account over a five-year period—taking taxable distributions as desired during that period—or "stretch" distributions over the lifetime of the inheritor by taking RMDs based on the life expectancy of the inheritor.[30] Taxes must be paid on the amount withdrawn in any year a distribution is taken.

3) Non-spousal beneficiaries who inherit an IRA on or after January 1, 2020 must liquidate the account within a ten-year period. This is a change implemented by the SECURE Act signed into law December 20, 2019 that (among other things) eliminated the tax-friendly "stretch" option.[31]

The new rule that eliminates the stretch IRA for some beneficiaries "completely changes the economics of the IRA," according to Bob Keebler, a CPA and founder of Keebler and Associates LLP, a nationally prominent tax advisory and CPA firm. It only makes mathematical sense, Keebler says, that taxable money withdrawn over a ten-year period is going to be taxed at a higher rate than that same amount of money withdrawn over twenty, thirty, or forty years.

To illustrate the difference, let's consider two different scenarios for a forty-five-year-old man who inherited a $500,000 IRA from his widowed mother.

---

[30] A non-spousal beneficiary who inherited an IRA prior to January 1, 2020, is "grandfathered" under IRA rules in place prior to implementation of the SECURE Act. The lifelong "stretch" option is no longer available for most non-spousal beneficiaries who inherit an IRA on or after January 1, 2020. Source: Ed Slott. Investment News. December 27, 2019. "The Stretch of the IRA is dead." https://www.investmentnews.com/the-stretch-ira-is-dead-175775

[31] The "stretch" IRA option remains available after January 1, 2020 for "eligible designated beneficiaries" (EDBs) that include spouses, minor children (until reaching the age of majority*), disabled individuals, chronically ill individuals, and beneficiaries not more than ten years younger than the deceased owner. *A child upon reaching majority age (eighteen in most states) becomes subject to the ten-year distribution rule. The EDB exemption applies only to a child of the deceased IRA owner and is not available to grandchildren. Source: Warner, Norcross and Judd LLP. December 2019. "The SECURE Act's Significant Impact on Beneficiaries." www.wnj.com/publications

In the first example, "Bill" inherits the IRA in late 2019. He has the option to take RMDs over the course of his lifetime with each RMD based on his life expectancy factor. Bill's first RMD will be $12,866 ($500,000 divided by 38.8, the life expectancy factor at age forty-five). His future RMDs will increase as his life expectancy decreases and the account experiences growth that has the potential to replace some or even much of the money withdrawn for RMDs.

Now consider Bill's situation were he to inherit the IRA on or after implementation of the SECURE Act on January 1, 2020.

Bill now must withdraw that $500,000 within a ten-year window. He had hoped to do so on an equal withdrawal schedule of some $50,000 a year, but he'll likely have to withdraw—and pay taxes on—more than that amount each year as the account experiences growth over the course of a decade.

In his first year alone, the difference in the two scenarios—taxes paid on a $12,866 lifetime "stretch" distribution versus a $50,000-plus equal schedule plan over ten years—is significant. Moreover, an annual non-stretch distribution of $50,000 or more could elevate Bill into a higher tax bracket. Extend that one-year difference over a ten-year period and it becomes easy to see how Bill will pay more in taxes under the SECURE Act rules than he would have if he could have stretched his tax obligation over a longer period.

As this book was being finished in early 2020, financial advisors were working with estate attorneys and CPAs to develop new strategies for dealing with the wealth transfer aspects of the SECURE Act. My office stands ready to explore such options, should you need help in this area.

Spouses who inherit a traditional IRA still have things a bit easier with an option—one of several available—to roll over the inherited amount into their own personal IRA and take required distributions based on their own life expectancy.

But the bottom line for both spouses and non-spousal inheritors is the same: Taxes must ultimately be paid on the inherited amount. Annual distributions may be required, and the penalties for failing to take them (or take the required amount) can be severe. The RMD concept might well be something new for younger inheritors who may know little to nothing of the rules. This is why we suggest visiting a tax professional—and we work closely with several—to fully understand your options and obligations when inheriting a qualified account.

This also presents another argument for the Roth IRA conversion strategy discussed previously. Keep in mind that assets in a Roth IRA can be inherited on a tax-free basis.

True, this strategy requires the original IRA owner to pay taxes on all money converted into a Roth. But in assuming the tax burden on qualified accounts that someday might be inherited, a parent who converts tax-deferred assets into a tax-free Roth IRA is providing what some people consider a legacy gift for their loved ones. Note, though, that under the new rules of the SECURE Act, an inherited Roth IRA also must be liquidated within ten years of the original owner's death. While Roth IRA distributions can be taken tax free, the new ten-year rule limits the amount of time the balance in the Roth can grow on a tax-free basis.

PROBATE: THE ESTATE PLAN FOR THOSE WHO DON'T HAVE ONE

No one likes planning for one's death, but the consequences of failing to do so can make life difficult for surviving heirs who must deal with the challenging aspects of probate.

Probate is the legal process that determines the distribution of our estate—and we all have some kind of estate—following our death. The inheritance process can be relatively simple for those who have planned for the distribution of their worldly assets to those they want to receive them. But probate can also be time-consuming and potentially costly for the heirs of people who failed to do such planning.

Let's examine that last unpleasant prospect first.

To die with no distribution plan in place is to die *intestate*. In this worst-case scenario, a probate court will determine the value of your estate, pay all taxes and outstanding debts from assets within the estate, and then determine how remaining assets will be distributed. The process of doing all this can take six months to more than a year, depending on the laws of each state and the complexities of the estate being settled. It also can involve appraiser, court, and attorney fees that must be paid before assets are distributed, hopefully to heirs or charitable organizations you want to receive them.

A WILL SHOWS THE WAY

A bare minimum way to help avoid this situation is to establish a will that spells out in advance your intentions for who gets what from your estate.

A will has the potential to make the probate process go more quickly and smoothly as it gives the probate court a documented statement of your intentions. Many professionally drafted wills pass through probate in a relatively short period of time. But this isn't always the case.

The will designates an executor—usually a family member or trusted friend—to administer the distribution of the estate according to instructions provided in the will. In most states, the executor presents the will to the probate court—a public record filing—and is given time to assemble and show proof of ownership of all property and securities as well as assess the value of those assets, and then pay any outstanding taxes and debts. Any creditor claims against the estate or challenges to the will must be made during this time. After all debts are paid and any disputes settled by the court, the executor begins distributing all remaining assets.

Estate attorneys with whom we work closely estimate the average cost of the probate process in Nebraska to be around $7,000 with the average length of the process to be around six months. Those cost and time estimates can be skewed considerably, however, by creditor claims or challenges from family members unhappy with their inheritance. Legal fees associated with lengthy probate battles have the potential to eat away large portions of an estate, and the time required to settle such cases can make loved ones wait for a year or more before receiving a dime.

IN TRUSTS WE TRUST

A trust is generally not subject to probate. Moreover, the estate holdings within a trust are not a matter of public record and are not subject to challenge by creditors.

A trust is a series of legal documents that, when structured and "funded" correctly, can generally distribute the assets of an estate in a timelier manner than is common in probate procedures. In many cases, estate assets within a trust can be transferred to heirs following the presentation of a death certificate.

Think of a trust as a safe with all elements of your estate locked inside. Also inside this safe are instructions for the distribution of these assets.

The combination to the safe is held by one or more trustees who are designated by the "grantor," the person or persons who established the trust. In many trusts, the grantors are also the first trustees, which means a person or couple who establishes a trust can have complete control of its assets for as long as they live.

Following the death of the original trustees, control of the trust goes to "successor trustees" designated by the grantors. These can be family members, trusted friends, or even the trust department of a financial institution. The successor trustee(s) is obligated to distribute estate assets within the trust according to instructions left by grantors.

A key to any trust is proper "funding." This means that all assets placed in the trust must be properly titled as property of the trust. Again, the trustees have control over how these assets are distributed.

It's important when establishing a will or trust to work with a lawyer who specializes in estate planning. That lawyer should also work closely with your financial advisor to make certain that all of your assets are either covered by the will or correctly titled to the trust. At Shunkwiler Financial, we work closely with several attorneys who specialize in estate planning.

POWER OF ATTORNEY, BENEFICIARY DESIGNATIONS

A couple final points that are important parts of any estate plan:

"Power of attorney" (POA) designations establish the right of people you trust to act on your behalf while you are alive but incapable of making decisions through physical or mental incapacitation. There are typically two types of POA designations—one to handle routine business affairs such as paying bills, and another to make essential medical decisions. POA designations, which are typically included as part of a trust, end upon the death of the person who established them.

A health directive or "living will," a legal document that establishes your wishes regarding end-of-life medical treatment, is another important component of legacy planning.

You also should do occasional reviews or updates to beneficiary designations on any life insurance policy, annuity, or other retirement account (IRA, 401(k), Roth IRA and others) that might be inherited. These designations can help transfer assets to heirs even when a will or trust is not in place. The same can be said of bank account Pay on Death (POD) provisions (which are not subject to probate), or Transfer on Death property deeds (available in Nebraska, but not in all states).

The bottom line on legacy planning: Be organized.

I can't stress enough how important it is for each of us to "put our affairs in order" while we remain able to do so. We all know of too many stories of grieving survivors having to search desperately for essential documents following a loved one's death. It doesn't have to be that way. The same kind of organization done in income planning applies to legacy planning, as well. It's a matter of assembling your assets and putting them in a place where the people you want to have them can easily access them when you're no longer here.

My earlier suggestion about having as many of your financial assets as possible under one umbrella is also appropriate here. It might also be easier on your survivors when they know they have only one financial professional or one estate attorney to contact in the difficult days after the passing of a loved one.

Making things as easy as possible for surviving loved ones may, in fact, be the ultimate act of legacy giving.

CHAPTER EIGHT

Pick Your Guide on the Pathway for Retirement

You've now explored what I consider the five core components of a successful retirement plan:

1) Developing an income plan that includes sources of sustainable lifetime income.
2) Continued growth of assets through a risk-appropriate investment strategy.
3) Implementing tax strategies to retain more of what you save.
4) Planning for future health care needs.
5) Establishing a legacy plan for your heirs.

Let's now wrap all this up with a quick discussion about finding the right guide down this Pathway for Retirement™.

CONSIDER A "DISTRIBUTION" ADVISOR

We talked at the beginning of this book about the difference between "accumulation" and "distribution" financial advisors.

Admittedly, many advisors can legitimately claim to be accomplished in both areas. But let's be frank here. Some advisors are more in tune with managing portfolios and selling products, the investment tools that help you grow wealth during the accumulation phase of life, than they are in helping you take income from those investments when you need it during the distribution phase that is retirement.

I believe that, in the years to come, you will need an advisor with a strong foundation of distribution strategies.

My company does offer the full spectrum of investment products necessary during the accumulation phase of life. But we've also developed an approach to taking this "utility drawer" of investments—all the stocks, bonds, mutual funds, bank accounts, annuities, IRAs, and insurance policies that you've compiled over a lifetime of hard work—and converting these investment tools into a tax-friendly retirement income designed to last as long as you do.

I once heard an advisor I admire compare this process to a symphony orchestra. Before a concert begins, each musician gets ready by tuning their instruments and "warming up," each musician often playing snippets of music disparate from each other. The whole process can sound like a cat fight. But then, the conductor brings everyone together to create beautiful, coordinated music.

An advisor who is as well-versed in distribution as in accumulation should be the conductor of your personal symphony. Such an advisor will take all the assembled pieces—each with a different role to play—and put it all together harmoniously.

Let's consider another analogy.

We love our college football here in Nebraska and understand how a team must have both an offensive and defensive coordinator. But ultimately there is a head coach who must make both sides operate as part of one team.

Your offensive coordinator may have done a fine job of being aggressive and building up your retirement assets. But the years just before and into retirement are the years you want to make sure your defense is very stout as well. This is the time when you don't want your offense to put your defense in a tough position through costly interceptions and fumbles. This is the time to protect yourself against market downturns.

As you consider your prospective head coach, put me in the camp that wants both the offense and defense to be equally fine-tuned.

FIDUCIARY RESPONSIBILITY

It's also my belief that the guide you choose should have a fiduciary responsibility. A "fiduciary," by definition, is someone who has both an ethical and a legal obligation to put the best interests of a client ahead of their own.

Now, this seems like a requirement you would expect from any financial services representative, but it is not required for all. Some brokers, agents, or others who sell investment products operate under a "suitability standard" that says they must consider only whether an investment product or recommendation is "suitable" to a client's needs. The idea of "what is in a client's best interest" can be considerably different from "what is suitable."

An Investment Advisor Representative such as myself has a legal obligation to act as a fiduciary. Brokers without an Investment Advisor Representative designation can offer investment products that might work for your individual situation, but such agents are sometimes restricted to offering only products developed by the company that employs them. Or, their recommendations might be influenced more by commissions available through the sale of one investment option over another.

At Shunkwiler Financial, we observe the higher standard that requires us to act in a client's best interest as opposed to the interests of a parent company.

INDEPENDENT VS. CAPTIVE ADVISOR

When I began my own company in 2011 after six years of working for a national parent firm, I was determined that my company would be a fully independent financial services firm.

Being independent lets my company explore investment opportunities and distribution options from the entire broad spectrum of the financial services industry. This is something I was limited in doing earlier in my career as a "captive agent" when I was restricted to selling the investment tools of the company that employed me.

Please don't misunderstand; they were perfectly fine investment products for many people, but they sometimes weren't as strong as other non-company options I knew to be available.

Today I strongly recommend that your guide on the road to retirement be a completely independent advisor who has access to the full range of investment and distributions options available in the search for products and strategies designed to work best for you.

YOUR PATHWAY TO AN ENJOYABLE RETIREMENT

Your retirement should be one of the most enjoyable times of your life. You've given decades of hard work to reach this point; you owe it to yourself to enjoy it.

Your retirement years are the reward for all those warm summer days you spent working when you could have been fishing, golfing, or just taking a leisurely stroll through the neighborhood. The reward for all of those cold, dark winter mornings when you reluctantly left the comfort of a nice warm bed to trudge through the ice and snow in order to get to work on time. Your retirement years should be a time to do the things you want to do as opposed to the things the working world demands that you do. They are the light at the end of the tunnel, the well-deserved payoff for years of sacrifice.

But to make these years everything you want them to be requires advance planning. This is where we come into the picture.

Your retirement will likely have unexpected twists, turns, and bumps along the way. Just as a guide is often helpful when hiking, boating, hunting, or fishing in unfamiliar terrain, so too is a financial guide important to show you the way down a road you've not yet traveled.

The first step in creating your Pathway for Retirement™ is establishing in advance a financial plan that provides for lifetime sustainable income, investment growth, dealing with taxes, and health care and legacy matters. This is how an individual person or couple can better prepare themselves for any detours they might encounter along the way.

CONTACT US

We invite you to step securely down this exciting path of wealth accumulation and smart distribution with guidance from our company's advisors on your personalized Pathway for Retirement™ plan. Give us a call, or send us an email. We're happy to help or refer you to someone who can:

402.466.3919
info@shunkwilerfinancial.com

ABOUT THE AUTHOR

Brett Shunkwiler, a native of Nebraska, began his career in the financial services industry in 2005 after earning his bachelor's degree in business administration from the University of Nebraska-Lincoln.

After six years of furthering his knowledge and experience with Ameritas, a nationally prominent financial services firm, Brett founded his own Lincoln-based company, Shunkwiler Financial, in 2011. His goal then and now is to provide clients the knowledge, attention, and time they deserve when planning their retirements.

As an Investment Advisor Representative who maintains a fiduciary responsibility to clients, he has passed the Series 6

(Investment Company and Variable Contracts Products Representative), Series 63 (Uniform Securities State Law), and Series 65 (Investment Advisers Law) securities exams, which allow him to provide financial and investment advice as well as manage investment portfolios.[32] He also holds an insurance license in Nebraska and several other states.

In his free time away from his company, he enjoys spending time with his wife, Lindsey, and three children, whom he coaches in baseball and basketball. He is active in church activities and is also an avid fan of the Nebraska Cornhuskers. For several years, he made regular TV appearances on a financial advice segment on Lincoln's ABC affiliate.

He is an active member of NAIFA, the National Association of Insurance and Financial Advisors.

---

[32] Series 6 (Investment Company and Variable Contracts Representative), Series 63 (Uniform Securities Agent State Law), Series 65 (Uniform Registered Investment Adviser Law). The Series 6 license allows the holder to register as a company's representative to sell mutual funds, annuities, and insurance. A Series 63 license is a state requirement of a person selling stocks, mutual funds, annuities, or bonds within a specific state. A Series 65 license requires a representative to have a fiduciary responsibility to clients when providing advice on regulated retirement accounts.

Acknowledgments

My first thanks always go to God, without whose blessings none of this could be possible.

This book also would not have been written without the help and guidance of my wife, Lindsey. She and our three children not only put up with me every day but also provide essential direction and purpose in my personal and professional life.

A note of thanks also to several financial professionals who made major impacts on my career. To Corey Poulosky, my first hiring manager and an early mentor in my time at Ameritas. To the advisors and authors at SHP Financial and to actuary Martin Ruby, whose thoughts and ideas have always made an impression on me. I've based much of what I believe on their philosophies, some of which are reflected in this book.

A special thanks to the professionals at Advisors Excel (AE), my Field Marketing Organization, whose advice and encouragement has helped me in the continuing development of my company and in the writing of this book. Special thanks to AE's Brady Lamar and Brad Johnson and their teams, as well as to Rick Dean, the editor of this book whom I met through my contacts at AE.

I also want to thank my team at Shunkwiler Financial, as they have been pivotal in the success of our company as well as in helping all of our amazing clients.

I would not be where I am today without the support of my parents, grandparents, brothers, and sister. They've always been there for me through good times and bad, and they helped shape me to become the man I am today.

Brett Shunkwiler
July 2020

www.ingramcontent.com/pod-product-compliance
Lightning Source LLC
Chambersburg PA
CBHW050242220526
45465CB00002B/520